The Real Estate

DATE DUE

Coach

Action
International

Business Coaching

Other Books in the Instant Success Series

Successful Franchising by Bradley J. Sugars

Billionaire in Training by Bradley J. Sugars

Instant Cashflow by Bradley J. Sugars

Instant Sales by Bradley J. Sugars

Instant Leads by Bradley J. Sugars

Instant Profit by Bradley J. Sugars

Instant Promotions by Bradley J. Sugars

Instant Repeat Business by Bradley J. Sugars

Instant Team Building by Bradley J. Sugars

Instant Systems by Bradley J. Sugars

Instant Referrals by Bradley J. Sugars

Instant Advertising by Bradley J. Sugars

The Business Coach by Bradley J. Sugars

The
Real Estate
Coach

BRADLEY J. SUGARS

McGraw-Hill

New York   Chicago   San Francisco   Lisbon   London
Madrid   Mexico City   Milan   New Delhi   San Juan
Seoul   Singapore   Sydney   Toronto

2 3 4 5 6 7 8 9 0   FGR/FGR   0 9 8 7 6

ISBN 0-07-146662-2

This publication is designed to provide accurate and authoritative information in regard to the subject matter covered. It is sold with the understanding that neither the author nor the publisher is engaged in rendering legal, accounting, or other professional service. If legal advice or other expert assistance is required, the services of a competent professional person should be sought.
—From a Declaration of Principles jointly adopted by Committee of the American Bar Association and a Committee of Publishers.

McGraw-Hill books are available at special quantity discounts to use as premiums and sales promotions, or for use in corporate training programs. For more information, please write to the Director of Special Sales, McGraw-Hill Professional, Two Penn Plaza, New York, NY 10121-2298. Or contact your local bookstore.

Library of Congress Cataloging-in-Publication Data

Sugars, Bradley J.
    The real estate coach / Bradley J. Sugars.
       p.   cm.
    ISBN 0-07-146662-2 (alk. paper)
       1. Real estate business—Handbooks, manuals, etc.   2. Real property—Handbooks, manuals, etc.   I. Title.
    HD1379.S93 2006
    333.33'068—dc22   2005025281

■ CONTENTS

■ INTRODUCTION

When it comes to your financial future, it's no longer as simple as work hard, put some money away, and hope for the best in your retirement years. In fact, retirement is no longer about your age or how long you've worked; it's about your ability to make and manage your own money.

As you're probably aware, many people have retired well before 60 and many have kept working into their 70s. So, what's the financial difference between these two groups?

Plenty.

There are literally thousands of ways for you to make money in this world, ranging from a basic job to your own career, or even your own business. And, while each of these strategies has its own merits, it's been shown that it's not how much you make or where you make it that matters most.

It's what you do with what you make that determines how wealthy you end up. Put another way, it's how you spend, or preferably invest, that determines your wealth and obviously your retirement age.

By the way, I'm not talking about your looking rich and being deep in debt. You know the people; they're in debt up to their eyeballs, have all the latest "stuff," but no real wealth behind it all. Ever met someone like this? More to the point, ever met that person in the mirror?

This is a book you really must read and follow.

Having a good job with a good, or even great, income is of no benefit at all, if all you do is spend or borrow more. Building wealth is about investing at least some of what you make in your future. And, when it comes to investing your money, most people are too scared to make a decision, so they either make no investments or put their money in the hands of a professional broker.

This book is about your learning how to make some of these decisions yourself, gaining knowledge so you can be financially literate and control your own future wealth.

If you're going to retire early, it's truly up to you.

And, as they say, retiring at 65 with just enough money to survive until you're 68 or 69 is not the way to end your life.

This book, and Brian and Sarah's story, is simple. And, while Brian and Sarah are not the real names of real people, the story is based upon coaching and teaching literally thousands of people how to create wealth through property investing.

If you follow the principles this book outlines, they'll work for you too. Of course, some will take more time to learn and apply, but maybe you will take less time.

You see, all too often we make things seem a lot harder than they actually are; we think rich people must be smarter than us, luckier than us, or have had rich parents.

The truth is becoming wealthy is not about anything more than learning the keys to success in the wealth game. And these wealth keys aren't secrets; they're tried and true principles that have worked over hundreds of years for many, many, many people—people who took the time to learn the simple keys and then went out and *did* what they needed to do.

As you'll learn from Brian and Sarah, it's relatively easy to know what to do; the challenge is getting out there and actually doing it.

The Coach will show you what to do, make each step simple, and get you on track to building your own property portfolio.

Remember this fact: how happy would you be if your great grandmother had bought 10 properties 80 years ago in downtown Los Angeles, London, Sydney, or Tokyo?

Investing is about your future—your family's future—it's not about tomorrow. Making money tomorrow is what your job or business is for; investing is about 3, 5, or even 10 years from now.

That said, yes, you will learn ways to make quick cash in real estate, but it's the exception rather than the rule.

Lastly, keep this one principle in mind: you don't have to be rich to invest, but you have to invest to be rich.

▮ MEET BRIAN AND SARAH

Brian had always considered himself a good, hard worker. He had a good education, was well-liked by everyone at the company where he had been working for the past 17 years, and he lived in a nice but average house with his loving wife and two teenaged children.

Life was good, but for some reason he had begun to question his finances.

He had a fairly large mortgage, but that didn't worry him much because the recent property boom had left him with a pretty solid amount of equity. He had some money in his retirement plan, and after all he wasn't even 50 yet.

Both he and his wife Sarah drove new cars. Yes, they owed a lot of money on them, but they had enough income to cover it.

They were both healthy and had a great circle of friends. What more could he ask for, he thought?

Unfortunately, the thought kept coming back.

He knew he was not entirely satisfied. When he was young he dreamed of becoming rich, a millionaire, but over time he'd faced his reality and assumed it was not for him, not for his family.

They were making good money, more than they dreamed of when they got married, but every time they made more, the expenses seemed to catch up.

He first noticed the feeling of unease soon after his forty-fifth birthday. It seemed to be in the pit of his stomach, and although he took no real notice of it at first, as the weeks passed he found himself paying more and more attention to it. He hadn't reached his dreams.

Sarah had brushed it off lightly when he first mentioned it to her.

"It's probably nothing more than a bit of anxiety, dear," she responded, her mind more on getting the children off to school than on what he was saying. The senior years at school were difficult ones for any parent, he knew, so he didn't push the point. Besides, she was probably right; she always was.

But it didn't go away. He knew there was more to it. Life at the office was just fine; there were no unusual challenges facing him or the company. Sales were up and so was profitability.

There were no unusual issues facing Sarah or her business either. She was also doing well. In fact they had begun calling the florist shop she owned and operated for the past five years a cash-making machine. Tapping into the convention scene had given her the edge she had sought for so long. The business now had a steady cashflow and she was no longer obliged to charge in line with her competition. She was at last enjoying the fruits of her labor.

Brian didn't believe that his children were the cause of his uneasiness either. Toni was a model daughter, an A-grade scholar, and a talented pianist. Ross was the cocaptain of the senior football team and wanted to enroll in business school after his graduation. They didn't smoke or hang out with the wrong crowd.

Baffled, he decided not to think about it anymore. He had far more pleasant and important things to think about, like his decision to buy the family a boat before the summer.

Now that was something that got his pulse racing! He had always loved the sea and boats. He had, after all, spent a few years in the navy after finishing school. Sarah said she didn't mind the idea of getting a boat; at least it would be another family interest and it would prove popular with their friends too, she knew. They had good credit, so of course they would get the financing.

Brian began to get more active about looking for a boat and started visiting some of the boat dealers and nearby marinas on weekends. He soon noticed that he wasn't as worried as he was before; at least he thought he wasn't.

Delighted, he decided the time had come to get serious about buying his cruiser. As with his cars, he would do this properly. That meant researching all his options to make sure he got the best deal possible.

It all boiled down to money, and as soon as he thought about it, he became aware of that uncomfortable feeling way down there in the pit of his stomach.

Could it be that money was a bigger problem than he wanted to accept?

Could it be that even though he had good credit and a reasonably good income, retirement was closer than he thought?

No, surely not. He was on a good salary and Sarah's business was going just fine. And in any case, all his friends were always complaining that the real cost of bringing up teenagers was far higher than at first met the eye. Not being able to make ends meet financially was part and parcel of having a growing family.

Anyway, retirement was a long way off, so he didn't have to worry about money—or did he?

When he got home from the office, he mentioned the tight feelings in his stomach again to Sarah. This time he had her undivided attention.

"Are you sure your health is OK, dear?" she replied after he had told her of how they had reappeared.

"As far as I know it is. But I could swear it's a little more intense this time around. The funny thing is it seems to come and go. It's only noticeable when the topic of money enters my mind. It's almost as if I have huge financial worries that I can't solve."

Sarah looked at him for a minute, deep in thought before replying.

"You know, Brian, we do have a lot on our shoulders right now. The family is probably at its most expensive, what with private schooling and sports and music fees to mention just a few things."

"I know, but that won't last forever. Before we know it the kids will be gone. At least we'll sleep easy knowing that we gave them the best start to life we could. But it's more than that," said Brian.

"I'm not arguing about that at all, dear," she responded. "The fact remains that we do have big costs. The mortgage soaks up plenty, especially as we are trying to pay it off a little quicker, and we are not getting any younger."

"What has that got to do with anything?" he retorted. He was starting to get a little agitated. The subject really pressured him for some reason.

"Remember, we decided to try to invest more into our retirement fund so that we wouldn't be a burden on the children one day."

"Yes, I know, and we haven't done any of it, but that still doesn't explain why I am getting these feelings in my stomach every time I think about money or finances. Remember when we were young how we thought we'd be rich some day? We were going to be millionaires."

Sarah sighed.

"Oh, I think it might just be a midlife crisis, and I know you keep saying it doesn't apply to you, but I think it does."

Brian shot her a cold glance, but before she could reply, he blurted, "Let's face it, Sarah; we are both getting older. I'm almost 50. We think we are fairly well off, what with the recent property boom and all the sudden equity we have in our home. But in reality, we could be doing a whole lot better than we are. We *should* be doing a whole lot better. I've worked 17 years and if I stopped tomorrow, we couldn't make our payments and we'd end up with nothing. It's like we're trapped!"

They sat in silence for a few moments, looking at each other.

After marshalling his thoughts and trying to change the subject, he said, "I hope you are right, Sarah. Because if you aren't, I think it will be time to visit the doctor, and that isn't a thought I cherish. Not at my age. The last thing I need is some kind of terrible surprise."

"Give it to the end of the month and see if it persists," she said. "Then make that appointment and get it over with. There's nothing worse than not knowing."

He nodded pensively, deep in thought. He knew he had to say something about their finances, but wasn't sure what.

"Sarah, I don't know if it's my imagination, but there seem to be more bills each month and even less money left over. It did cross my mind that if the unthinkable were to happen and I were to get sick, be unable to work or something, we would be in deep trouble."

Sarah looked over to the side table in the entrance hall and sighed. They had always placed all the incoming mail that needed to be attended to there; it was a habit they developed when they got married.

Brian followed her glance.

"See, that pile does seem to be getting bigger, doesn't it?" he commented, not really expecting an answer.

"Mmmm," she replied, and fell silent.

Sarah noticed Brian's moods had begun to change. He had become a little more sullen and less spontaneous. Yet it didn't worry her. She instinctively knew that it had more to do with the much talked about "midlife crisis" than anything else. The children had remarked on it too. But at least he hadn't gone and done something silly like one of his friends had.

They had known Jess and Mary since school days and had stayed good friends ever since. After all, their lives had virtually been exact replicas. They had both married their childhood sweethearts, they had gone to the same school, they both married in the same year, and they were each other's best man. Jess and Mary also had two children, who now were following in their parents' footsteps and were good friends with their children.

Jess, they often said, hadn't coped with middle age too well. He came home one day with a Harley Davidson motorcycle. Beautiful bike it was, but he had never before shown any interest in bikes. Mary nearly threw him out. They had one almighty fight over that bike. He insisted on riding it every Sunday morning, but she never once went along. She had dug her heels in and refused point blank. And he wouldn't back down either; he had always had a stubborn streak in him.

That incident severely tested their marriage. At times it didn't look like they would make it.

Brian really admired the way Sarah had handled the whole episode; Mary confided in her and they worked through each challenge one day at a time. Sarah helped her deal with Jess's crisis constructively and sensibly. It saved their marriage, he knew.

But all that was in the past now and so too was the Harley.

Then one day, this letter arrived.

Sarah could hardly contain herself as she read. She had always been the one to open their mail.

"Rosewood High is having its first reunion and you are invited!" she read aloud as she made her way over to where Brian was sitting.

"Oh, honey, this is going to be so much fun. We simply have to go."

"You bet we will," he replied. "I wonder who we will bump into?"

"Even more interesting is whether we will recognize them," she laughed.

"Or them us!" he responded, and they both had a good laugh.

Talk of the reunion dominated their discussions from that moment on. Brian was really excited by the prospect of bumping into people he hadn't seen since leaving school. Sarah too found herself thinking back to what she and her school friends did during those carefree days; if only they had realized at the time how carefree they were.

"I wonder if Rose will be there. She was that old-fashioned girl who looked like she belonged in my grandmother's class!"

Brian laughed loudly.

"And what about that girl who you used to go camping with? You know, the one who was a good athlete?" he asked.

"You mean Belinda?"

"Yes, that's the one. You were quite friendly with her, weren't you?"

"Yes, we were. I really don't know why we lost contact. I think she had a baby soon after leaving school. Last I heard she was a single mom. I guess we had nothing more in common at the time."

Brian hadn't noticed that his stomach pains had disappeared.

"Oh look, Brian, there's Jim," Sarah said as they entered the old school hall. "Remember him? He was the captain of the swimming team."

"Well, I'll be" Brian exclaimed. "Doesn't look at all like the cool, well-built athlete I remember! He's fat and bald."

They both chuckled as they made their way to the noticeboard that displayed the seating arrangements for dinner.

"Look at who we're sitting next to, Brian," Sarah exclaimed. "Belinda!"

"That's great. We were just talking about her the other day."

They made their way over to the table and were surprised to see Belinda already seated.

"Belinda, how are you?" Sarah shouted as she ran the short distance to the table.

"Remember me?"

The tall slender girl looked up in surprise.

"Sarah? Is that you?" she asked, a broad smile spreading across her pretty face.

"Yes, it is. You look beautiful. How have you been? Oh, remember Brian? We are still together after all these years."

The two old friends hugged warmly; there was so much catching up to do. Brian was more than happy to talk with them. He was fascinated by what was unfolding. He was beginning to remember more and more about Belinda as they talked. Slowly snippets of information and memories sprang to mind.

But, it was time for Brian to go catch up with a bunch of his old buddies.

It was more than an hour later when Brian saw his wife was still sitting with Belinda, so he ventured back to join them. He couldn't help but notice how Belinda seemed so confident, so strong.

She had never struck him as coming from a wealthy family before, but the more he looked and listened, the more he began to realize that she was indeed a wealthy woman.

The jewelery she was wearing, the perfume she used, the designer clothes, and her imported shoes all pointed to the fact that she was more than just comfortably well off.

She had to be loaded.

"So who's the lucky man, Belinda?" Brian asked, unable to contain himself any longer.

"No, there is nobody," she replied, looking a little startled at first. "You see, although I have done well for myself, the fact remains that I am extremely poor in that area of my life. I never was lucky enough to meet Mr. Right. After I gave birth to my daughter, men seemed to lose interest in me. In fact, I was certain they were avoiding me like the plague at the time. But then again, I guess the last thing most young men needed in their lives at the time was a girlfriend with a baby."

"I'm so sorry to hear that, Belinda. I never knew. I suppose I just assumed that we all got married and had kids, just like in the movies."

"I got over it years ago, Brian. I guess I diverted my attention by diving headlong into real estate. I set myself the goal of becoming a millionaire by investing in the real estate market, and that's just what I've done. I sometimes think I simply don't have the time to find the right man anymore."

Brian was amazed at what he was hearing; he wanted to ask so many questions.

"Why real estate, Belinda?" he continued. "Why not the stock market?"

He was glad he had found something to contribute to their conversation.

"That's a really good question, Brian, and I'm glad you asked it. See, my

Coach once told me that many companies on the stock market invest their surplus capital into real estate. They buy property. They deduct all the expenses they can first, and then, as a shareholder, you get what's left. Check the fine print in company quarterly and annual reports—you will be amazed what you find.

"Also, I really wanted something I could do part-time. You know, I had to work, take care of my daughter, and well, try to become rich. Funny thing is, real estate has taken very good care of me."

Brian was becoming more and more interested with every word, but it was Sarah who asked the really interesting questions, and this surprised him. He had no idea his wife was so interested in investing.

"You were always a great athlete, Belinda. We really admired you for that. But what strikes me now is that over the years you don't seem to have lost any of that competitive drive that you had as a champion all those years ago," Sarah said. "You seem to me to be treating your investing like a game, and that's something I find intriguing. Is that intentional?"

"Absolutely, Sarah. Not only does it make it more pleasant, but it makes sense too. It has all the same elements of a game, like rules, players, spectators, and the score. I find it helps me keep my eye on the proverbial ball, so to speak. But there I go again using sports terminology!"

Before they had stopped laughing, Belinda continued: "As you know, I was not the brightest kid in the class. So how did I succeed in real estate? I got myself a Coach and he taught me everything I needed to know."

"You're kidding," Sarah quipped.

"Not at all. I could never have done it on my own. See, I met my Coach at a football game many years ago. I was invited to his corporate suite as a guest with a friend, and the rest, as they say, is history."

"So what sorts of things did he teach you?" Brian asked. "Must be very technical, investing in the real estate market."

"That's the beauty of it, Brian. It's really not rocket science at all. My Coach has this amazing ability to explain things in simple terms. But that's not all; he also has developed these simple to follow rules that make it really easy to win the real estate game."

Both Brian and Sarah were fascinated with what they were hearing. If she can do it, then so can we, Brian thought. He knew his wife would be thinking along similar lines.

"So tell me then, Belinda, who is your Coach?"

"Why, would you like to meet him?"

Brian couldn't believe his ears, nor his stomach; there was that familiar throb.

It was a few weeks later when Belinda finally called.

Brian was all excited. "Will he see us, and can we learn from him like you did?"

"Yes, Brian, he will be back in town in a few days and he's agreed to meet you both, but I can't promise anything. He's strict."

"What do you mean strict?" Brian's heart began to beat a little faster.

"You know, like any good Coach, he's tough and is only willing to work with people who are serious about playing the game as hard as he does."

"But how will I know if he wants to coach us, and why would he coach us? I mean he doesn't even know us."

"Brian, the Coach is wealthy, so he doesn't need the money. He does this as a hobby, and he's coming to see you as a personal favor to me. He hasn't taken on any new students in many months. But don't worry, I know he'll like you; just be on time."

Brian and Sarah arrived at their favorite coffee shop early. They had a quick look around as they walked inside, eager to see whether Belinda was already at a table. She wasn't.

They quickly made their way to the back of the room and settled down at a quiet table in the corner. They didn't particularly want other customers to listen in to what they were going to talk about.

The young waitress came over and asked if she could get them anything.

"No, not just now, thanks; we are waiting for two other people to join us. Then we'll order."

No sooner had the waitress disappeared when in walked Belinda accompanied by a tall, immaculately groomed but casual man. She spotted Brian and Sarah and headed their way.

"Hi guys, I'd like you to meet my Coach. Coach, this is Brian and Sarah."

They stood and shook hands, then resumed their seats.

"So, Belinda tells me you were all at school together," the Coach said. "You must have had a great time together. I have found her so much fun to work with."

"Yes we did. Only she must have taken things more seriously than we did, because look where she is now!" Sarah joked.

"Oh, come on . . ." Belinda interjected. "You two have made a wonderful success of life. Aren't they just meant for each other, Coach?"

He smiled, and asked why Brian and Sarah had wanted to meet him.

"Since our school reunion, Sarah and I have been doing a lot of soul searching," Brian said, a little nervous. "It has become quite obvious that unless we do something really serious about our financial future, things might not turn out like we dreamed. We really aren't as financially secure as we would like; in fact, we are a lot shakier than we first thought. That's why we have decided to ask you if you could coach us into acquiring and building a real estate portfolio."

Brian felt like he'd just finished a race.

The waitress reappeared and took their orders. When she returned and handed out the coffees, the group was already deep in discussion.

The Coach was testing Brian and Sarah, making sure he wasn't going to waste his time teaching people who would pull out halfway, or not apply what they learned each week.

Brian was sweating and Sarah had almost worn a hole through her pants from squirming. Brian made his case and the Coach listened as he and Sarah answered the questions.

Finally the Coach agreed; he was convinced that both Brian and Sarah were serious about learning his property investing rules.

It was a full hour later that they rose and headed for the door, pleased with the progress they had made. The Coach had agreed to coach them, and Brian and Sarah were excited, yet scared stiff.

"We'll see you next Tuesday at 11 then, Coach," Brian said as they shook hands.

"That's right. You sure you know where my office is?"

He and Sarah nodded.

The
Real Estate
Coach

Part 1

■ Follow the Rules

As the clock struck 11:00, Brian pushed open the door to the Coach's office and gestured to his wife to walk in. As the door swung closed behind them, the Coach appeared from his inner office, smiling.

"Good to see you two," he said, hand outstretched. "Come on into my office and take a seat."

Brian glanced over to Sarah as they entered; he clearly liked what he saw.

The Coach took a seat at the large round table that filled half of the ornate office. His new clients followed his cue and seated themselves. It was just as well that it was a comfortable office, Brian thought. They were going to be spending a lot of time here.

Brian could immediately tell that the Coach was highly organized. He watched as the Coach picked up a manila folder from a neatly stacked pile on the desk and handed it to Sarah. Together they read the label on the front cover.

Follow the Rules

"You know," the Coach began, "it always amazes me how many people just dive straight in and buy their first investment property before they have stopped to think about the big picture. I mean, most people seem to just want to get a foot in the market before they even have a half reasonable idea of what they ultimately want to achieve, how they are going to achieve it, what structures they need to set up, and what principles they will use to guide them. And the real scary thing is that most of them don't even seem worried that they haven't gotten the basics in place first. If the truth be known, they probably wouldn't even know what the basics are."

He stopped and cast a careful eye over his new students, eager to see whether what he was saying was making an impression.

"If there's one thing I want to impress upon you today it's this: Don't, whatever you do, fall into this trap and make the same mistakes that the vast majority of so-called investors do."

He paused to let that sink in.

"My main message today is to follow the rules. Follow the rules and you'll find it's really quite simple."

Sarah nodded as she glanced over to her husband.

"Now you both have good incomes, right?" the Coach paused as they both said yes.

"So, does a good income equal rich or even plain old wealthy?"

Sarah jumped in, "Probably not, but it helps."

"Great answer, income rich doesn't mean you have wealth behind you. You see, simply put, the aim of working is to *not* have to work."

The Coach went on before they could ask any questions.

"You make money from a job and should put some aside to invest over time; the more you put away and the better you invest determines how long you have to work before your investments will pay for your lifestyle."

"But Coach, we have no surplus; we are always paying our bills," Brian felt embarrassed as he said it.

"Brian, that's exactly why you need to start investing. Put simply, you don't need to be rich to invest, but you have to invest to be rich."

Sarah was busy taking notes but lifted her head to ask, "So, you're saying we can retire early?"

"Great point, Sarah. Retirement is a function of money, not age. If you have enough invested you can retire at any age; problem is people would rather buy the latest shoes or watch or perfume on a credit card than buy an investment property. That, my friends, is going to have to change."

Brian knew that they could easily cut back in a few areas. In fact, he'd thought about it before but really had no goals that meant he *had* to do it.

"The basic idea of becoming wealthy is to first develop your cashflow through your job or your own business, and then to turn it into physical assets that in turn produce a cashflow all of their own."

As Sarah turned the page in her folder she noticed the Coach had already printed some notes for them.

**Turn Cashflow into Physical Assets—
The reason I invest in property is to turn my cashflow
from my job or business into an asset that grows in value
and gives off cashflow of its own.**

"We all think we know what an investment is," the Coach began. "We use the term almost every day. People talk about investing in property, shares, art, stamps, coins, antiques, and vintage cars. But which of these are really investments?"

Brian looked up quizzically.

"What do you mean, Coach? Surely if you buy something with a view to selling it sometime in the future for a profit, then that's an investment."

The Coach settled back in his chair and ran his fingers through his neatly groomed hair.

"It really all comes down to what we do with these things we 'invest' in," he continued, emphasizing the word *invest*.

"What do you mean?" Sarah asked.

"Understand this: Most people focus on only the first part of my definition for an investment. As long as it appreciates in value, then they regard it as an investment. They are concerned only with the projected capital value of the item they have bought. But here's the real point. A true investment must also produce cashflow along the way. It must produce an income stream while it's increasing in value. See, most investments only increase in capital value slowly. There are exceptions, of course, but in general, this is a longer, slower process."

Brian nodded; he could see where this was leading.

"One other thing: most people who regard themselves as fairly familiar with investing also make the mistake of believing it's just about a return *on* investment. They seem to think that as long as their investment is producing a cashflow of, let's say, 11 percent a year, they are doing well. But I say you need to ensure you get a return *of* investment first. You need to be sure your initial outlay is safe before you begin receiving a return *on* your investment. Far too many people have invested in dubious schemes based on a healthy projected return on investment, only to find they lost their initial outlay after they had banked the first few returns. Does that make sense?"

Both Brian and Sarah shook their heads. Again Sarah found the Coach's note first.

**The Coach's Definition of an Investment—
An investment is an asset that both grows in capital value
and gives off passive cashflow.**

The Coach stopped Sarah from jumping ahead in their notes as they discussed the next lesson.

"It's important to clearly understand why you want to invest in property in the first place," the Coach said. "If you don't, then you run the risk of disappointing yourself."

Sarah was thinking she knew what the Coach was talking about; it had been her one concern about entering the real estate market as an investor.

"Decide on your outcomes up front and then you will be in for no surprises. See, you buy an investment property for one of two reasons only: capital growth or cashflow."

"What do you mean by that, Coach?" Sarah asked.

"Either you go for the long-term value in the property—what you will be able to sell it for in years to come—or for the income it will produce for you week in and week out from the time you bought it."

"But can't you have a property that is good for both, Coach?" Sarah asked.

"You'll find it's usually one or the other, Sarah. See, a good income-producing property will usually be found in a lower socioeconomic area, and these properties don't usually appreciate that much in price. Capital growth properties, on the other hand, are those in more prosperous areas. They usually don't attract a great rent, but they will appreciate nicely in the long term. When we get to discussing building your property portfolio later on, I'll show you how and why you need to buy both types of properties."

"Now, out of those two reasons for buying property, you've got to remember that one of them is far more important than the other; can you guess which one?"

Brian had already turned the page and guessed right with capital growth, but then the Coach asked him to explain why.

"Not really sure, Coach," he replied.

"Well, at its most fundamental, your job or business brings in the income, and your property investing is where you get that money you make to grow over time."

Here's what Brian had read.

Income versus Capital Growth—
The reason I buy property is essentially for capital growth,
but sometimes I have to buy properties with higher
cashflow to balance my portfolio. Income from property is
designed to cover costs while my property grows in value,
not to generate a substantial cashflow.

"Let's look at the rules that will guide you as you invest in the real estate market. The thing to bear in mind is that there is a difference between an investment and a speculation. A huge difference. So what is that difference?" he asked, and leaned back in his chair. His question was met with blank stares.

"Well, the difference is that when you invest, you do so in accordance with a set of rules. Remember, follow the rules."

Both Brian and Sarah nodded.

"You see, most investors are really gamblers, they have no set plan and no set of rules to follow, and they make investing choices based on quick decisions. This is nothing more than speculation at best, and I want you to become investors and high-quality ones at that.

"There are in fact three sets of rules you need to play by. These include the overall rules of the game, your own rules of the game, and specific rules for the specific game you are playing at the time."

Sarah got ready to take more notes. She knew the Coach was about to elaborate.

"The rules of the game are the general rules as laid down by the government, local authorities, banks, legal institutions, real estate agencies, and local conventions. You have basically no control over these rules."

Sarah was grateful she knew shorthand.

"Your overall vision, mission, goals, and objectives will determine your rules of the game. They will be established according to your overall situation and circumstances. They will reflect your modus operandi, ethics, morality, wishes, and desires. You set these rules, and you can change them. If you do decide to change your rules, first check with a mentor or someone whose opinion you respect, to see if it is really your rules you need to change, because the environment you operate in has changed, or if you are just becoming lazy or careless."

Brian was writing as fast as he could but was thankful that he had Sarah to rely on if he fell behind.

"Your specific rules for the specific game you are playing at the time will vary according to which marketplace you are dealing in at that moment—whether you are dealing with an inner-city unit or an outer suburban refurbished house. They could also vary according to which city you are dealing in and whether you are buying a house to live in yourself or one that you are buying for capital growth only. Again, these are your rules and you can change them to suit your situation."

Sarah was impressed.

"Now I understand the value of having a set of rules, Coach. I can appreciate how important they are."

"And they become even more vital when you consider that you could be playing many games at the same time," the Coach continued.

"You could be investing in different markets. Generally speaking, there will be different rules for the following types of properties: inner city units, inner city houses, fringe city units, fringe city houses, outer city units, outer city houses, satellite units, and satellite houses."

"In addition, there are different rules governing new units, existing units, and refurbished units as well as new houses, existing houses, and refurbished houses."

Brian whistled in surprise.

"Each market is different," the Coach went on.

"The investing rules for buying a new inner city unit are quite different from those that apply when buying an existing house in an outer city suburb. Then there are rules for property you intend living in yourself, property you intend renting out, property you want to buy and then sell again quickly, property you intend holding onto long term, property you aim to get capital gain from, property you're buying for a rental purchase plan, and property you're buying through vendor finance deals. In fact there are about 27 different types of residential real estate categories—I like to be involved in several of these at a time."

"Between now and next week, I want you to go and look at 11 houses at open houses or such and start to see what's for sale and what's rented," added the Coach as he glanced at his watch indicating their hour was complete.

Both Brian and Sarah felt mentally exhausted by the time their first session ended. They also felt strangely stimulated. The Coach smiled as he showed them to the door; he had seen this countless times before and knew they had the makings of great real estate investors.

As they got to the car, they saw the last page of today's notes.

> **Investor versus Gambler = Rules—**
> **Investing is about following a set of investment rules;**
> **anyone without rules is more of a gambler than an**
> **investor. As an investor I need to learn enough to develop**
> **and follow my own set of rules.**

Brian was amazed at how quickly the week had flown following their first session with the Coach. Sarah had felt drained; such was her intensity in their session. She remarked to her husband that it had reminded her of the first time she had signed up with the gym all those years ago.

Brian, too, had felt the difference. He had never felt better; his stomach pains seemed to have become a thing of the past and that relieved him. He had stopped beginning to fear for the worst.

They found themselves looking forward to their next session so much so that it began to dominate their discussions. This, they agreed, was a good thing, as it drew them closer together by giving them something in common to become passionate about.

They were discussing this when the Coach opened the door in response to their knock.

"Hello, Coach, how are things?" Brian asked as the door opened.

"Good to see you two," he responded. "Come on in."

He led them to his office and beckoned them to their seats. He handed them their folders for the session, and outlined the main topic on the agenda for the session.

"It's a strange thing, but the more you know, the better the decision you can make," the Coach began. "It all comes down to the quality of your teacher or mentor. See, the better your teacher, the better the knowledge you will have. And the better your knowledge, the more informed you will be, which will enable you to ask better questions and thus make better decisions. This will, in turn, have an impact on the actions you take and the results you get."

Brian nodded. This was, after all, quite logical, yet he could see right away that it was probably one of the main reasons he hadn't quite achieved all he had dreamed of.

"When you are investing in high-cost commodities like real estate, you really want to minimize your risks because mistakes here can be very costly. Most people simply can't afford to make too many mistakes, can they?"

Sarah nodded. This was the major worry she had about becoming a real estate investor.

"So how do we ensure that we won't be taking too many risks then, Coach?" she asked.

"By doing your homework well," he replied. "And by that I mean you need to be getting out in the market, becoming an expert in what is happening. You need to inspect at least 50 properties before you begin negotiating 10 of them. And of that 10, you'll only negotiate an agreed deal on 3 and probably receive finance for just 1. That's the level of activity you need to be aiming for."

Brian whistled in surprise, as he knew how hard it had been for them to get to see just 11 properties that week.

"Think of it this way: If you inspected 50 properties, you'd soon get a good grasp on the market in that particular area, wouldn't you? You'd quickly get to know what good value is and what isn't. You'd also get to know which agents are good and which aren't."

"We'd be starting to minimize our risk," Brian responded.

"That's absolutely right," the Coach replied.

"As with any profession, job, or skill, the more you do of it the better you get. Buying real estate is no different; the more you see, the more you know. The more people you ask for ideas and advice, the better your decisions will be. And so on."

The Coach directed them to the first page of this week's notes.

> **Risk Equals Lack of Knowledge—**
> **People who don't know what they're doing take big risks**
> **when they invest. The more knowledge I have, the more I**
> **reduce my risk when investing in property.**

"You'll remember from our last meeting that I refer to investing in property as 'playing the game.' If you want to get into real estate investment, you have to abide by the rules of the game. Every game has rules, and playing the property game is no different."

Brian nodded and smiled. Sarah had always accused him of being more interested in sports than business.

"The first thing you need to do is understand the rules of the game you are playing. See, imagine what would happen if you went to watch a football game and only one team knew the rules. The other team wouldn't stand a chance, would they? They would be taken to the cleaners."

Brian nodded.

"It's the same with property investors, isn't it?" the Coach continued. "If they don't know the rules of the game they are playing, they will lose big time, won't they? I have seen far too many people make expensive mistakes simply because they didn't know what they were doing."

He paused to let what he had just said sink in.

"And remember, there are different rules you need to know depending on what market you are investing in. The rules can also be different in different countries and states. Local governments also have their own rules—for example, when subdividing blocks of land and building townhouses, the rules can differ from city to city."

Sarah completed her notes and asked: "So, Coach, it's up to us to find out what the rules are depending on what we want to do in real estate? I mean we need to really do our homework well before we take the plunge and start buying."

The coach smiled. "You learn fast, Sarah."

"So how do we find out what the rules are, Coach?" Brian asked, beginning to feel the slightest hint of that old stomachache once more. Must really be connected to stress, he thought.

"That's where having a good team on your side comes in," the Coach replied. "Talk to estate agents, lawyers, building contractors—anyone you think may have the information you are looking for. And even if you don't know what you are looking for, still go see your team. Show them what you are planning and ask them what you should take into consideration. Get talking—and really listen."

After a short pause to let them complete their notes, the Coach continued.

"Generally speaking, local government rules around the world are fairly similar. You pretty much need a permit for everything you want to do. It's important that even as a novice investor you understand that you have to follow the rules, rather than try to beat the system. Remember, rules are made to be followed," said the Coach with a wry smile as he had them turn to their notes.

The Game's Rules—
Every game has its own set of rules, and every state, county, or even country in the world has different property investment rules and laws that I have to learn to follow.

"Now that we have discussed the rules of the game, we need to think about yet another set of rules that you must obey if you are to win the real estate game long term," the Coach began. It didn't surprise him that both Brian and Sarah had a look of astonishment in their eyes.

"What other rules can there possibly be, Coach?" Brian asked.

"Think back for a minute, Brian. Why are you doing this? What is your motivation? And what will ensure that you meet your goals?"

There was a short silence before he replied rather hesitantly: "You mean our own rules?"

"That's right, Brian. Your own rules. See, you need to bear in mind that there is a difference between investing and gambling, or as some refer to it, speculation. What's that difference, Sarah?"

She thought for a minute and then replied: "The difference is that when you invest, you do so in accordance with a set of rules."

Both Brian and the Coach nodded.

"Remember the three sets of rules you need to play by. The actual rules of the game, your overall set of investing rules, and your specific rules for the specific game you are playing at the time."

Sarah knew the Coach was about to elaborate, so she had her pen ready.

"The rules of the game are the general rules as laid down by the government, local authorities, banks, legal institutions, real estate agencies, and local conventions. As I've already shown you, we have no control over these rules."

Sarah was feeling a little like she was back at school.

"Your overall goals are what we're working on here. Everything from the level of return on investment you're after to the basics of what risk levels you are willing to take on, and even how you agree that an investment is right for you to be able to make an offer. You see, the structure you build here when there is no emotion, while you are at home and not even contemplating an investment, will save you when you get to an auction and your emotions and desire to 'win at all costs' kicks in."

Brian was starting to understand the Coach's structure.

"Some things you want to focus on are your goals and whether you are after capital gain or cashflow, whether it's a long- or short-term gain you are after, and how you will structure your investments and the things that will cover you entire investing future."

Sarah was pleased that she was following so easily.

"Now I understand the value of having a set of rules, Coach. I can appreciate how important they are," she explained.

"Great stuff, so onto the third set of rules. You've already looked at your overall rules, and now we need to get specific. You see, if you were going to invest in businesses you would need a set of business investment rules, but as we are discussing real estate, you need a set of real estate investment rules."

"Remember, I mentioned that there are more than 20 main types of property deals. Generally most people find their niche in just one of these. It could be shopping centers, or condos, or developing vacant land, or where most novices should start out, residential houses."

"And you could be buying them for long term, for short-term renovations, or for long-term land value to be able to build condos or townhouses on them. It's really your choice."

"Of course, I recommend that you buy and either just hold or renovate and hold for new investors, but we'll get into a lot more detail over the coming weeks about that."

Brian piped up with a question: "So Coach, how much detail do we have to have, and what if we don't know enough to write our rules yet but want to invest?"

"Great questions. First let's deal with the level of detail. Generally you'll find you have between 8 and 15 rules; any more than that makes it too hard to find properties that meet your requirements, and any less makes it too easy."

"As for wanting to invest before you have your rules decided and written down, that's simple: invest in more knowledge so you know what rules you should have. It's quite often that people ask me what they should invest in and my only recommendation is for them to get more knowledge so they don't have to ask such a question."

"Think about this: As you get better at investing you'll start to be involved in several deals at once. Your rules become even more vital when you consider that you could be playing many games at the same time." The Coach continued, "You could be investing in different markets. You could also have different requirements at a particular point in time; for instance, you might be after developing some cash quickly so that you can build up a property portfolio that will increase nicely in value over time. If this were the case, you'd be looking for something you could buy cheaply to renovate and resell. It really all depends on what your requirements are at the time."

"So, just so I'm crystal clear, how is having a set of rules going to help, Coach?" Sarah asked.

"Think of it this way: if you were on the lookout for a cheap property with potential to make a quick profit, would you be tempted if you came across a great place that was just perfect—say the type of place you could see yourself living in someday?"

"Well, I guess so," Sarah blurted.

"No you wouldn't, or at least you shouldn't, because that wouldn't be the type of property that would generate some quick cash for you! If you followed your rules you'd pass on this occasion and keep looking."

Sarah still looked troubled.

"Why would we do that, Coach? I mean, if we come across a bargain, shouldn't we snap it up while we have the chance?"

The Coach shook his head.

"No, because by doing that you may not be able to accomplish your goal, which was to build up some cash so that you could buy something with capital growth potential. You see, by deviating from your plan you become sidetracked and lose sight of what it is you are doing this for. You would run the risk of never succeeding in building up a portfolio of appreciating properties in the long term.

"One of the reasons for rules is to take that short-term gain emotion out of the game. And, on this specific example, always remember you are not buying a home for you to live in; you are buying properties for other people to live in. Never let your own likes and dislikes cloud your judgment."

Sarah understood. She could see where the Coach was heading.

It was time for a break, and everyone got up to stretch and get a drink, but Brian was really thinking hard about what he would have invested in if he hadn't met the Coach. It probably would have been that boat. He knew the Coach had already impacted their net worth for the long term.

As they sat back down with fresh drinks the Coach began again.

"What we are going to look at now are the types of property deals that you can do. You see, they will figure in your rules when you go out looking for properties to buy. So what are the different types of deals, then?"

Brian looked up at the ceiling for a while, and then replied: "I have heard about negatively geared deals, Coach. Is this what you mean?"

"Exactly. Any idea what the other two are?"

"I guess one would have to be ones that produce cash quickly, Coach. You know, the ones we have just been talking about."

"That's right. They are quick cash deals and the third type of deals are positive cashflow deals," the Coach continued.

"Let's look at them one at a time, shall we?"

Sarah turned to a clean page in her notebook.

"Negatively geared deals are those that make a week-to-week cash loss or more commonly a paper, or after-tax, loss. They are usually found in high-value, high-capital-gain, low-rental-yield return areas. By this we mean they are top-class properties in high-class suburbs, but the rental returns are never going to be in the 1.6:1 bracket. What's the significance of this? Well, if the rental return is 1.6 times the purchase price per $1000, the property will usually pay for itself. If it's better than 1.6:1 it will pay for itself and should generate a cash surplus. Negatively geared properties are more likely to be in the 0.8:1 bracket. As an example, on a property that cost you $400,000 you would expect to achieve a rental return of $300 a week. Low rental returns usually need to be compensated for with high-capital-growth properties."

Sarah nodded as she wrote.

"A low-rent area is one where the ratio of rental return is lower than you'd get from a lower-class suburb. Just because the property goes up in price doesn't mean the rent goes up correspondingly. Example: In this type of area, a $100,000 property might rent for $150 a week, and a $200,000 property might rent for

$250 a week. Therefore, two $100,000 properties will bring you $300 a week combined, yet a $500,000 property will probably earn you only $350 a week.

"I know this seems crazy, but it's partly about supply and demand. More people rent at the lower end of the scale than the higher end."

"And, with a negatively geared capital growth property, you might break even with cash, but still make a paper loss. You also need other highly taxable sources of income for negatively geared property deals to be of any benefit."

Brian stretched back in his chair; the going had been tough but at least he knew Sarah would have copied down most of this.

"With positive cashflow deals," the Coach continued, "the rental income you receive is more than all the cash expenses you incur added together. You still get the paper tax deductions, so you would usually make a cash profit, but after deductions break even on paper. These deals usually involve lower-value, lower-quality, high-rent properties. They are the ones that often don't give you high capital gains, but they will always produce higher rental returns to compensate. They are the properties you buy for their regular income, not their rocketing capital growth prospects. Now you will still get capital growth with these properties, but commonly they are at lower growth levels than the negatively geared or capital growth property. Capital growth on a positive cashflow property is still vital over the long term but is not the prime reason you put this type of property in your portfolio."

It was Brian who now spoke.

"Coach, aren't these deals called positive-geared deals?"

"Brian, there are positively geared deals, but this is not what I am referring to here. This type of deal is all about *cashflow,* not gearing. I am talking about properties that produce a positive, and taxable, cashflow. They might still be positively geared, or produce a positive return after all deductions, but it's the cash we want to measure."

"Ah, I see. Thanks."

"Quick cash deals, on the other hand, are those where we buy a property purely as trading stock. The primary purpose is to buy and sell the houses, not to invest in them for the long term." He stopped as he saw Sarah wanted to speak again.

"So, Coach, that would be like in my business where I have stock that I buy and sell?"

"Exactly, but in the property game, if we get stuck with a couple they won't decrease in value; we will still get cashflow and they should still grow in value over time." The Coach really wanted to stress the next point.

"The one thing you must not do here is buy too many, or overcommit and not be able to hold onto them for the medium term."

Sarah nodded while she wrote.

"With a quick cash deal, we buy the properties, spend some money fixing them up or changing their basic use—they could need a coat of paint, a new kitchen, or some new carpets, an added bedroom, or even something more substantial—and then sell them again. We reinvest the money we make into other deals."

"What is the real purpose of such deals, Coach?" Brian asked.

"It's the quick cash deals that can get you going in the first place, or speed you up along the way," the Coach replied. "These deals can also be used to help generate more, or larger, down payments for other deals."

"I understand," Brian said, and turned the page.

"Bear in mind that quick cash deals don't have to be restricted to property. Some people I know buy and sell cars to generate cash to finance their next property deals or renovations.

"Remember though that quick cash deals require more knowledge and generally more skill and experience than do the longer-term investments."

The Coach offered his students another glass of water and poured one for himself as he told them of their added homework on researching a start on their own rules.

Your Own Rules—
There are literally hundreds of strategies
for property investing. I need to develop my
own investing rules within my niche.

"It's well known that people buy on emotion and not logic," the Coach explained. "And real estate agents are well aware of this. Just look at any advertisement in the property section of the newspaper and you'll see what I mean. It's all about location, location, location as the saying goes, and for good reason. Location is an emotive consideration. When did you ever see an ad that highlights return on investment, capital growth, or functionality?"

Sarah knew exactly what he was talking about.

"But it's so easy to get caught up in the emotion when you are looking at a property that interests you, Coach. I mean how can we stay cool, calm, collected, and focused on the logic?"

The Coach smiled, took a long drink from the glass on his desk, and then said, "That's where your rules come in, Sarah. It's by sticking to your rules that you will ensure you stay focused on the logic and not get caught up in the emotion. And don't forget, the selling agent will be trying all he or she knows to get you on the emotional level."

Brian was paying a lot of attention because he instinctively felt the wisdom of what the Coach was saying.

"This is the main reason I am very careful when I buy at auction. See, when you think about it, the entire auction process relies on the fact that the bidders get swept away by emotion. That is why many end up paying way more than they originally intended, just to win."

Sarah completed her notes, looked over towards Brian, but addressed her question to the Coach.

"So when we buy investment properties, we need to keep to our game plan.

What if we still get excited and let the agent think we are buying on emotion? Shouldn't we play their game?"

"No, absolutely not, Sarah. Ever heard the saying you are what you think? You will run the very real danger of losing your way and buying something not in your game plan, or overspending. But let me tell you this: Ever wondered what response you'll get if you were to talk to a real estate salesperson on the logical level?"

Sarah looked interested, but did not venture a reply. It had, after all, been many years since she and Brian had bought their home.

"I'll tell you the response you'll get. You'll most likely get a blank stare and loads of guff; then they'll change the topic to something on the emotional level. See, almost all real estate salespeople have no training for the investment market. Their property managers may have been trained, but they hardly ever get involved in the sales process. They only come into the picture once you have bought and are ready to appoint someone to manage it for you."

Brian nodded.

"Remember, your job is simply to buy based on the return you will get, and this is determined by your game plan. Your rules will have been developed to ensure you stick to your game plan. Get it?"

Both Brian and Sarah nodded.

"It all seems so logical, Coach," Sarah quipped, and they all laughed.

"That's about it for this session, folks. Next week we will take a look at the reasons behind your game plan—your goals. We will then be thinking about developing your game plan, or plan of action, as it is otherwise known."

It had been a huge session and both Brian and Sarah were beginning to feel exhausted. They were actually pleased they had reached the end of the session. Gathering up their notes, they thanked the Coach and made their way to the door.

"Looking forward to next week already," the Coach said as he opened the door. He knew he was stretching them. With both the learning and their homework of looking at more properties and starting to develop their own rules, they would be busy. The Coach also knew that it was when they were outside their comfort zones that they would learn the most.

Emotion versus Logic—
I must continually remind myself that I must buy on logic and *not* emotion. It's one thing to have a set of buying rules; it's another to be disciplined enough to follow them.

Brian wasn't one for plans; he understood the reasons for them and he had always done them at work. Yet when it came to his private life, about the only thing he planned was what sports to watch on the weekend.

This had been a sore point with Sarah. She had always thought that Brian didn't take life seriously. That was the reason why, as she often pointed out, they were still struggling financially even though they both had good incomes. He, of course, refuted that, responding that he didn't plan to fail, he just failed to plan.

So they both thought their next session with the Coach would be rather pertinent. They were both more than just interested in seeing what the Coach would teach them on this topic.

"Nice to see you both again," the Coach said as he ushered them into his office.

The first 20 minutes of their session was taken up by going over the properties they had seen and explaining just how much they were learning about real estate in their area from the agents and people they were meeting.

The Coach listened intently but knew time was slipping away, so he brought everyone back to the point of today's lesson.

"Today we are going to be getting down to the fun stuff—we will be setting goals and developing a plan of action."

Sarah could hardly wait. She loved conceptualizing and visualizing. She also loved documenting. This would be "her" session, she thought.

"Any idea why we need a set of goals when setting out to invest in the real estate market?" the Coach asked. "Why couldn't we simply get out there and hunt for something that looks reasonable, and when we find it, put in an offer like everyone else does?"

It was Sarah who was quick off the mark.

"Because then we would be gamblers and not real investors, Coach," she replied.

"Yes, that's right, Sarah. But what would be wrong with that if it brings you results? I mean, if it works for others, why wouldn't it work for you?"

This time she wasn't quite so quick to reply.

Seeing that there would be no response, the Coach continued: "See, if you were to do the same things as everyone else, you would expect to get the same results that they do, wouldn't you?"

They nodded in agreement.

"And what results do most people get when buying investment properties? They get pretty ordinary results, don't they? See, what we are aiming for is not ordinary results; we are aiming for outstanding results. Most property 'investors' end up asset rich and cash poor after just a few purchases when the banks won't extend them any more credit."

More nodding.

"So to ensure we enter the market sharply focussed on what we want to achieve at the end of the day, we need to set and then write goals that will guide us when we are in the thick of the action."

The Coach paused to let what he had just said sink in.

"It's important that we set SMART goals."

"What do you mean by SMART goals, Coach?" Sarah asked.

"Ah, I was wondering whether you would ask that, Sarah. A goal is said to be SMART if it is Specific, Measurable, Achievable, Results oriented and has a Time frame."

He paused while she wrote.

"The goal must be specific—for instance, we are going to build one property wealth wheel a year consisting of two negatively geared properties and three positive cashflow properties. We will raise the financing to get started by doing a quick cash deal. Don't worry about the how to's at this time; we will go into it in greater detail later."

Brian was thankful Sarah was good at setting goals; he knew he would struggle to get it down on paper.

"The goal must also be measurable because you can't manage something you can't measure. You need to know when you have achieved it and this you do by measuring. Measurements also tell you how you are progressing, how close you are to hitting the mark."

"The goal must also be achievable. It is pointless setting a goal you know you can't achieve. Why set yourself up for failure? In addition, goals must be results oriented, which means they must embody a result. For instance, it's no use saying you want to buy more property so that you will be better off financially. What does that mean? Better off compared to what? And how will you ever know when you have reached that point? This type of goal contains no result."

"Finally, the goal must have a time frame. By when must you have achieved the goal? I think you will probably find that every goal could be achieved if you were to wait long enough."

Sarah completed her notes but didn't look up. She knew there would be more to come.

"Your homework is to think about what you want to achieve through building a real estate portfolio. Once you have done that, I want you to set yourself some SMART goals, so then we can set about developing your plan of action."

It was a quick set of lessons but probably the one they needed to focus on the most.

That day Brian and Sarah went home feeling elated. They were finally taking steps that would, with the assistance of their Coach, lead to a better and more secure long-term lifestyle.

They talked a lot over the course of the next few days. They debated what they wanted to achieve and by when. And they wrestled with the concept of SMART goals.

After what seemed like ages, they finally agreed on what their goals would be. They were satisfied that they were at least thinking along the same lines, but they were anxious to see what the Coach would think. Sarah switched on the computer and began to type.

Our Goals—

1. To buy our first investment property within nine months, i.e., by the end of October this year.

2. To build up a $30,000 working fund by selling our second car and canceling our vacation this year.

3. To start by buying a modest property that we can renovate and sell for a profit. This will help us increase our working fund so that we can reinvest in a property that we will rent out.

4. To buy at least one property a year for the next five years.

5. To stick to residential property and not get involved with units, apartments, or commercial property.

6. To develop sufficient passive income from our property portfolio so that Brian can retire 10 years from now.

Setting Goals—
The only way I can make good decisions on which way to go is to know where I am going. I need clear SMART goals: Specific, Measurable, Achievable, Results Oriented, and with a Time frame.

Brian and Sarah at last felt like they were beginning to make progress. They had some good goals in place. Sarah had said this was more than Brian had done in all the years they had been married. Deep down he knew she was right.

"Well, how did it go with your goals?" the Coach asked as he began the next session.

"We think we have done well, Coach," Sarah replied. "We certainly did a lot of soul searching."

She handed him the sheet of paper and held her breath. He quickly read through it and smiled.

"Excellent, you have both done well. At least you have made a start. You have a clear idea of what you want to achieve and how you envisage going about achieving it. Now what you will be doing is developing a plan of action to get the ball rolling. Life is truly about having a dream, turning that dream into SMART goals, and then planning the actions you need to take to make your dreams and goals a reality."

Brian beamed with pride and satisfaction. He knew he was operating outside his comfort zone. And amazingly enough, it was rubbing off at work, too. More focus at home had made him a better employee.

"I want you now to begin developing a plan of action that will get you moving. You need to think about the specifics of getting into the real estate market now."

Sarah looked puzzled.

"But, Coach, we don't know enough yet to develop a plan."

"If you wait until you know enough, you won't ever get moving," the Coach responded. "You need to at least plan the basics. This plan will, of course, change as you go along, but you need to make a start."

"We have already done that, Coach," she said. "We are here learning, aren't we?"

"That's my point," the Coach replied. "Coaching must feature in your plan of action. So in it, plan for your coaching sessions. Include them. And start planning for other activities like getting to know your chosen market, getting to know the rules of the game and writing down your own rules. See, you have actually made considerable progress so far, but unless you take action, all this knowledge will be of no use. So plan to use it."

He let sink in what he had just said.

"Think of the plan of action as your road map. It is the map you must follow to achieve your stated goals."

As they discussed the actions involved in looking at and evaluating deals, Brian found himself daydreaming about his plan and how much of a challenge it would be to do the work.

"So, Brian, what else do you think you'll need to do?" the Coach questioned, noticing Brian's distant thoughts.

"Sorry, Coach, I was just wondering when I'll get time to do any of this."

Sarah shot a look that could kill at Brian. He quickly started to wish he hadn't asked the question.

The Coach smiled before making sure Brian understood. "Brian, I'll make this simple. Rich people do what poor people aren't willing to, and if you want the rewards, my friend, you have to do the work."

It was the end of their session. Brian and Sarah left after saying their good-byes. The next week would not be an easy one for the couple as the pressures of their home life, their business, the kids, and their newfound "hobby" were beginning to take their toll.

That's why the call from the Coach was even more important.

"Brian, it's the Coach," he began. "I just want you to know I think you have what it takes. Believe in yourselves; I believe in you both." And he hung up as quickly as he had started.

Brian was both stunned and impressed, and he knew it was time to get his plan on paper.

**Develop a Plan of Action—
I need a good plan that I can act on now, rather than
waiting for a great plan and never taking action.**

Part 2

■ Balance Your Portfolio

Brian knew they were making steady progress; they had established clearly what their goals were and they had made a start on their plan of action. The ball had started rolling. They were looking forward to the next phase of the game, which the coach had told them revolved around gathering more knowledge. This, he explained to Sarah, was part and parcel of learning how the game worked.

They found themselves looking forward to their next coaching session so much that it made the days drag. Of course, their homework kept them busy, and eventually the day did come when they found themselves seated in the now familiar office.

"Most people understand only two basic philosophies for investing in real estate," the Coach began.

"You buy a property for the cashflow it will give you, or you buy a property for the capital growth it will give you."

So far, so good; no real surprises there, Brian thought.

"Rental income is a great reason for investing in real estate," the Coach continued.

"Consider this: even though $5000 a year in rental income on a $100,000 property is only a 5 percent yield, that doesn't worry me. You see, I love tenants because they pay off the property for me. I use tenants to pay for a percentage of the property's expenses while I collect the capital growth."

The Coach cleared his throat and continued: "Statistics for the last three decades show that around 60 to 70 percent of the population of most major western countries own their own homes. But let's look at rental statistics. Over this period the number of renters has grown from around 20 percent to now around 30 percent. This is a global trend. Again, this is a fairly constant figure in percentage terms, but with the growth of the global population, the number of rental households over this period has approximately doubled in most countries. That means there has been an unbelievable demand for new rental properties. Millions of new rental properties have come onto the market over the last 20 years. The vast majority has been supplied by private investors like you and me!"

It was now Sarah who had a question.

"There will surely be times when we have no one in the property paying us rent, Coach. What do we do then?"

"Let's examine this carefully. Around the world, in most major cities 10 percent is a very high vacancy rate for rental properties. Yes, some have been higher, but most often it's lower.

What this means is that 90 percent or more of all the rental properties are filled with paying tenants. Generally, properties that are overpriced or badly kept are the ones that stay vacant for any length of time. So, basically, you don't have to worry. Vacancy is manageable, workable, and most important, insurable," the Coach replied.

Sarah was nodding as the Coach continued.

"I just want to remind you of my main point, that rent is not how I measure the quality of a real estate investment; it's just one of the numbers we need to know. Rent is what pays some of our costs as we collect the long-term capital growth."

Brian had a point that was bugging him. "So, Coach, with positive cashflow deals, do we buy them for the extra cashflow or what?"

"Well, it's important to know that your portfolio of properties and wealth needs to grow overall. To keep it growing, you need to keep your cashflow, your capital growth, and your borrowing capacity all growing together. So, some properties that have a higher cashflow and are what we call positive cashflow deals are vital to balance your portfolio of deals."

The Coach's notes on the subject read:

Cashflow—
A property that has relatively low capital growth usually
has a higher rental cashflow. Investment properties that
generate a greater cashflow can usually be found in lower
socioeconomic areas, outer suburbs, country towns,
and in some high-density housing.

"Let's turn our attention now to capital growth properties, the ones that generally produce a negative tax position or even a negative cashflow. Technically they're called negatively geared deals."

"And what would these typically look like?" asked Brian.

"The types of properties that typically fall into this category are ones in a top position with assured capital growth. You have to give up good cashflow because you should be getting a solid capital growth rate. But one point I need you to understand is that growth needs to exceed the cash contributed each week or month to cover the costs of owning and paying off the property to make this type of deal worthwhile."

"So, the first deals get good cash but lower growth, and these deals get good growth but low rental cash returns?" Sarah confirmed more to herself than the Coach.

"Exactly, but just because a deal is negatively geared, meaning that after your tax deductions it makes a loss, it doesn't mean it can't be cashflow positive."

"I never knew that," Brian quickly slipped in. "So I can own a property, and after I pay the mortgage and taxes and other costs, I can still have some money left over from the rent, but after I complete my tax return, the government still allows me to collect a tax refund?"

"Yes, that's definitely possible, Brian. You are not going to get a positive cashflow property that has huge capital growth very often, but they are out there, so keep your eyes peeled," the Coach responded.

"I regularly find that the only people that can't find positive cashflow or even solid capital growth properties are people who don't believe they exist. It never ceases to amaze me how many people handicap themselves by their own ignorance."

"So where then should we look for such high-capital-growth properties, Coach?" Sarah asked.

"Look for them in top positions like a riverfront or waterfront, river views or water views, on a hilltop with good views, city views, or adjacent to parklands, state or national forests or reserves. Look for properties that are in unique positions or are unique properties in other ways, be it a high-growth coastal resort or in a high-class, 'old money' suburb."

Sarah was taking notes as he spoke.

"You will still want to buy well, though, and you don't want to have much renovation work to do on it, if any. I'd also recommend you buy after a period of no growth or at the lower end of the market."

"That brings me to one of the most vital points about the difference between cashflow deals and capital growth deals. Can either of you guess what it might be?" the Coach questioned as he took a sip of his water.

Brian and Sarah looked at each other but nothing came to them.

The Coach took a serious tone as he made his next lesson come to life.

"The big difference between a positive cashflow deal and a capital growth deal is that cashflow is regular and happens week in and week out, year in and year out. But capital growth is totally unpredictable; it can happen steadily each year, in spurts, or even stay flat or downward over a number of years and then leap massively in a 12-month period. That's why balancing your portfolio is imperative for your long-term investing strategy." The Coach handed them another note as he finished.

Brian made one more point: "So, Coach, is that why most people don't like investing in property, because it's not predictable?"

"Probably very true, team, very true. But therein lies the benefit to those with knowledge. Imagine that your great grandmother had bought 10 houses on the water in any major city in the world 100 years ago. I think you'd agree that when thinking about capital growth it is hard for us to 'know' what will happen, but that said, the past is usually a good indicator."

Capital Growth—
Properties with a higher capital growth usually produce
a lower rental yield. Properties in high-class suburbs,
on water, with views, and close to the city usually have a
higher chance at capital growth.

"Property offers the investor excellent tax advantages in many countries around the world," the Coach began. "Paper losses associated with depreciation are totally tax deductible. Tax deductions make investing in real estate a very attractive option. The government can't afford to provide housing for everyone, so they give you and me a tax deduction as an additional incentive to provide it for them."

Brian nodded to Sarah; this was something they had discussed before.

"When you purchase a property, you are buying an asset made up of a number of items that are all wearing out over time and will eventually need repairing or replacing. The land, of course, is the exception to this. Most governments allows you to claim a number of 'paper deductions' by having your accountant write off a percentage of the value of each 'capitalized' item each year at rates prescribed by the tax office. These items include the building and its fixtures and fittings such as carpets, curtains, fences, garage doors, waste disposals, spa pools, decking, and air conditioners, to name just a few."

"Along with writing off a part of the value of the building and its contents each year as what's called depreciation, most governments also allow you to deduct 100 percent of the tax-related expenses for a property within the tax year such as rates and local taxes, insurance, property manager's fees, mortgage interest payments, property seminar costs, subscriptions, building repairs, and any other expense that directly relates to your property investment."

"As I've mentioned, one of the stunning things about real estate is that often when rental income exceeds all expenses and you get the property paying you weekly positive cashflow, you also receive a tax refund!"

"Can you explain more about how is this truly possible, Coach?" Brian asked.

"Here's an example. Let's say we negotiate the purchase of a three-bedroom house in one of the outer suburbs of a smaller city. The people really need to sell; it's only a couple of years old and we pick it up for $90,000, and its real market value is about $112,000 based on what other houses are selling for in the area. I use equity in my own home to secure a 100 percent mortgage of $93,000. You'll see that I've allowed $3000 for costs of buying the property and even some local taxes, as some states and countries will charge you these. And, to make it very real I'll pretend our loan is at 6.5 percent interest on an interest-only loan."

"So, we won't be paying back both principal and interest then, Coach?" Sarah asked.

"Correct. Then I engage an appraiser, or in some countries you might call him a quantity surveyor/chattels valuer to complete a Valuation Report where he details the original building construction cost at $45,000. Because it is two years old and the previous owner claimed some of the costs over those two years, I start with a depreciated book value of $42,778 that I can start depreciating at 2.5 percent a year. He also produces a book value of $17,100 for the fixtures and fittings, which can be depreciated at an average of 11.25 percent per annum. Remember, in some states and countries these rates are higher or lower than others. The property rents for $160 a week, so here's how the numbers look."

He handed them his next handout.

Rental Income	$160 per week	$8,320
Mortgage Interest	6.5% Interest Only	–$6,045
Rates or Local Taxes		–$600
Insurance		–$350
Repairs		–$300
Total Expenses		–$7,295
Positive Cashflow		**$1,025**

"100 percent financed, this property has paid us positive cashflow of $1025 for year one, and the exciting thing is it's tax-free! Here's how."

He gave us his next handout.

Depreciation—Building	$42,778 @ 2.5%	–$1,069
Depreciation—Fixtures & Fittings	$17,100 @ 11.25%	–$1,924
Total Income	Rent @ $160 per week	$8,320
Total Deductions (including depreciation)		–$10,288
Tax Loss		–$1,968
Tax Refund	@ 30% (your tax rate)	$590
After-Tax Cashflow		**$1,615**

"Once we have deducted depreciation, we have created a tax loss on paper. If we had purchased the property in our name and we pay income tax on our wages, at a tax rate of 30 percent, we can then claim a tax refund of $590. If our tax rate was 40 percent, then the tax refund would increase to $787.

"The exciting thing in this example is that we bought the property at a discount, we have received positive cashflow, a tax refund, and have not even considered what the capital growth could be. Let's assume it grows at just 5 percent per annum and calculate our total return from this deal in the first year."

He handed out another sheet of paper for their files.

Equity Gained at Purchase	($112,000 – $90,000 = $22,000 – less costs)	$22,000 – $3,000 = $19,000
Positive Cashflow		$1,025
Tax Refund	@ 30%	$590
Equity Growth	At Capital Growth of 6% of the $112,000	$6,720
Total Year 1 Return	**Cash + Equity Earned**	**$27,335**

"Now, I know this is a little more detail than you are used to, but by the end of our coaching you will easily be able to work these numbers on any property you look at so you can tell exactly what sort of return you'll get."

"Wow, Coach, I think that stuff is a lot easier to follow than I thought it would be," blurted Sarah.

"Sarah, that's great. A good Coach makes things as simple as he can for you, so hopefully it's working."

"Back to the lesson. if you look at the notes you'll see a property investment pays you up to four ways, if you buy right and structure it correctly for tax. But don't make the mistake that thousands of property investors around the world make. Don't buy an investment property just for the tax benefits it provides. Look at the tax benefits as welcome fringe benefits that just happen to be around at the time. Focus on the cashflow or the capital growth the property produces, not the taxation."

Sarah slid the sheet of paper into her folder as the Coach was talking.

Taxation—
My plan needs to be built on the fact that both I and
my advisors understand my tax obligations and benefits.
But I must never buy an investment property purely
for the tax deductions I may get.

Both Brian and Sarah now understood the reason for increasing the value of their investment properties. They also understood that if they could increase the value of their investment properties, then not only would their property be worth more intrinsically and attract more rent, but they would also be able to borrow more.

This had been discussed at length during the week at just about every opportunity and it certainly was a topic that they were both excited about. Yet the more they discussed it, the more they convinced themselves that the Coach would have some surprises for them when they next met.

They were right.

"OK, so what happens when I get three negatively geared properties and I want to buy a fourth? I'll tell you, the bank says *no,* you don't have the ability to service the loans," began the Coach.

"This happens all too often with novice investors. They end up asset rich and cash poor and even compound the mistake by putting in an extra few dollars a week to try to pay the mortgage off even faster."

"The aim of today's session is to help you see what steps you need to take to keep your borrowing power intact as you grow your investment portfolio."

"So, Coach, what happens to those people who seem to overcommit on negatively geared properties? Sarah asked.

"Usually they end up having to sell one of the homes when the market is not great to free up some cash. It's a pity because if they had planned it a little better, everything would have been financially much better off.

"So, before we get into the details, what do you think is the simplest and most powerful lesson here?"

"To invest in both positive and negative cashflow properties so you keep it in balance," Sarah leapt in before Brian could get his answer out.

"Great thinking," the Coach was impressed. "Brian, anything to add?"

"Coach, I would just say that you need to make sure you can keep the serviceability of the loans solid, not just the level of debt."

"Another very solid point. Your LVR, or Loan to Valuation Ratio, is one thing the bankers will want to know, but the other and equally important thing is the cashflow from both your rental income and your own incomes to make sure you can pay back the monthly repayments fairly easily.

"Now that that's settled, what I want to do is to give you a good example of how you can increase your borrowing capacity as you go." The Coach was ready to change focus.

"There are many other ways to increase the value of your property deals, and we'll get into more of them in future lessons, but the obvious one is to renovate and rent. As an example I'll run through some scenarios I use to good effect."

Sarah flipped to a clean page in her notebook and got ready to write.

"I'll use smaller numbers so we can make the math easy, but the same applies to bigger deals as well. This first method is very useful, and I've had students use it to turn $40,000 into $120,000 in one year. This is how you do it.

"Start off with $40,000 and aim to use it to buy an $80,000 unit or house. Remember, this could easily be $400,000 for an $800,000 property. To achieve this basic deal, though, the bank will want me to put down 20 percent of the value as a deposit. That's $16,000. They will then lend me $64,000.

"OK, so out of my initial $40,000, I've spent $16,000 on the deposit. I then allocate $18,000 for renovations and a further $2000 for transaction and legal costs. That leaves me with $4000 liquidity from my initial $40,000 to cover any unforeseen problems. So far, so good?"

"Yes, I follow," Brian responded. Sarah nodded.

"Now, if I paid $80,000 for a property it should have been worth at least $90,000 already and through bargain hunting and negotiation I bought it well. This value property that has had $18,000 spent on it wisely should increase in rent by around 20 to 30 percent and then in value to around $120,000 in most areas.

"I then organize a revaluation with an appraiser who is approved by the bank through which I want to refinance. Once the valuation is complete I refinance the unit, and borrow the 80 percent that they will lend me on the new $120,000 valuation. That's $96,000. I pay off the $64,000 loan at the same time, and I get $32,000 back. To this I add my $4000 left over from my initial $40,000 funds. That gives me $36,000. I've now gotten almost all my money back from the property and I still own the unit."

Brian whistled in amazement.

"This gives me two options. Add it to my real estate portfolio if the rental figures stack up or sell it as a quick cash deal. Because it usually takes one month to renovate a property, one month to sell it, and one month for the sale to settle, if I really focus I can repeat this cycle four times a year doing quick cash deals.

"On this deal I will make $20,000 profit when I resell the unit for $120,000. Add this to my initial $40,000, which I recovered from the sale, and I now have $60,000 to play with when I buy my next property.

"Using the same basic criteria as before, I buy, refurbish, refinance, then resell the second and make another $20,000 profit. Only this time, once I have recovered my initial $60,000, I now have $80,000 to play with on my third purchase of the year. I now have enough in the kitty to allow me to buy two properties this time and not just one. Same scenario again results in a $40,000 profit when I sell, and I get $120,000 to finance my next round of purchases. I now buy three properties of similar value and land up with $180,000 after they have been finally sold. Along the way I will have outlaid somewhere in the region of $40,000 in commissions, duty and other related expenses, leaving me with a profit of $140,000 for the year."

Brian liked what he was hearing. They were now well and truly into the meat of the subject. This is what it was all about.

"Now, I don't want you getting ahead of yourselves here. It usually takes a few years of practice and doing one deal a year for people to get good enough to manage that many deals at once, but hopefully you get the point of how it starts working and why managing your borrowing capacity is all-important."

"Coach, it seems so simple, why don't more people do it?"

"Well, Brian, simple doesn't mean easy; there is a lot of work involved in doing this, as well as a lot of knowledge you will need to gain, but I'm sure you'll agree that the rewards are going to be worth the effort.

"Now, method two involves hanging onto the properties I've just bought and not selling them. I keep my stock. Here again, I spend one month renovating the property before going back and getting it revalued. I then refinance and use that money to acquire the next property."

This made more sense to Sarah. It was the option she had always imagined property investors would use.

"This I can do up to 6, 8, even 10 times a year, with the result that my initial $40,000 will end up purchasing me around $1,200,000 in property a year (10 properties at an average property valuation of $120,000)."

"That's not a bad year, Coach," she commented.

"Yes, but remember that this is when you get better at it, not right away. And there's more," the Coach continued. "Remember, each property only cost me $100,000 after renovation and I got almost all my cash money out. That means I have $200,000 in equity (10 properties at $20,000 equity per property) and I still have approximately the $40,000 I started with."

Brian whistled to himself.

"In effect we have now turned $40,000 into $240,000 in 1 year. A 600 percent return. But I must stress, you two are nowhere near ready to play the game at that level yet, though you will be in a few years with practice. Like Belinda, your time will come."

"Is this a popular strategy among investors, Coach? Is this what Belinda does?" Sarah asked.

"Well, no and yes. Most people don't do this simply because they believe it will be too much work, but yes this is the strategy Belinda has followed all along. Now of course she's doing much bigger deals, but she started out on very simple deals. In fact, she lived in most of the houses as she renovated them herself to start with.

"Also, many that try to invest this way run out of borrowing capacity because they didn't make sure to structure their purchases intelligently."

"Just goes to show, doesn't it?" Sarah said, leaning over to Brian. "We really have been working hard but we only get paid for our work once. Investing pays us for the work we do once, forever."

The Coach was glad the lesson of leverage was starting to pay off: do the work once and get paid forever was one of his mottos.

"Method three is a little more complex but even more powerful than the previous two," the Coach continued. "It hinges around investing the original $40,000 into a fixed deposit or treasury account at the bank. The bank will again lend me $64,000 on 80 percent security of the $80,000 property.

"But this time I ask for a more than 100 percent loan instead, using my cash on deposit and the property as security, so I borrow $104,000 for the purchase and any buying costs. Now stay with me on this; it's very powerful once you become a seasoned investor."

"So, Coach, we borrow the entire purchase price plus the renovation costs and don't pay a deposit to the realtor?" asked Brian.

"Correct. You'll need to work with a good private banker to get this running, but it works. Here's the way we work it from there."

"I renovate with the rest of the loan money and then return to the banker a month or two later to get the property revalued."

"So, Coach, the revaluation will be about $120,000 if I've done it right and presto, the banker will release my cash as a deposit or security and I start all over again," Sarah almost jumped as she spoke.

"Sarah, I think you're a genius! Just remember that at the start you won't need to get so fancy. In fact, put away your notes on this until you're up to about your fourth house and then you'll really understand what we've just gone through and how you can use it."

"By the way, in a moment you'll see why we do this, but keep bank fees in mind as we go through it."

Sarah was writing madly once more.

"The beauty of this method is there is no refinancing, taxes or other costs. This is because I am just releasing my collateral. I am not selling or refinancing the property; I simply renovate, release, and let it sit in my property portfolio."

Brian really liked the simplicity of this strategy. He sat back in his chair, satisfied. It had been a good session. And the funny thing was that he didn't feel as emotionally drained after it as he usually did. He could quite easily face another full coaching session there and then.

**Borrowing Capacity—
I want to borrow as much as I can and leverage
up my investments. If I don't balance my portfolio,
I will run out of borrowing capacity. If I play the
game right, the more I invest in property,
the greater my borrowing power becomes.**

"Ever wanted to own a money tree?" the Coach asked as they settled down on their chairs at the start of their next coaching session.

They nodded.

"Who hasn't?" Sarah replied.

"Now I know that's just not possible, but there is something very similar. It's a wheel that spins money out forever," the Coach went on.

"That's right. It's a wheel that, once spinning, will produce a constant income stream no matter what."

Both Brian and Sarah looked at the Coach in surprise. They sat there in silence, waiting to hear what he would say next. Surely this would turn out to be a joke.

"What I'm going to show you now is how to put the theory you've learned so far into practice. I'm going to reveal to you the secret to creating amazing wealth through investing in residential real estate."

Sarah smiled. Brian felt the beginnings of a stomachache coming on.

"The Property Wealth Wheel could be the most powerful concept you will ever learn. And it's amazingly simple. It involves all three different types of property deals that we have already talked about."

Brian smiled to himself, flipped to a clean page, and prepared to write; this was the stuff he liked best; working models that he could use. He stopped when he noticed the Coach was about to pass around another handout.

"The Property Wealth Wheel is a simple concept—it consists of just three components: negatively geared (capital growth) deals, positive cashflow deals, and quick cash deals," the Coach began.

Brian glanced at the handout; it was so simple and graphic.

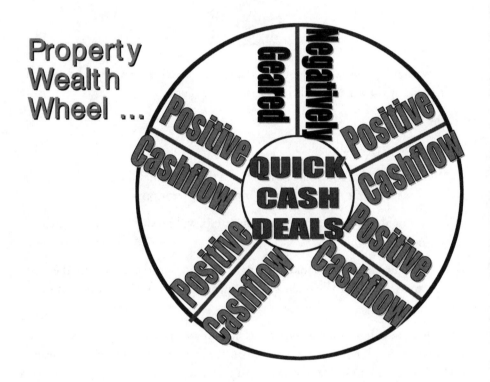

"The wheel, like any other device, needs to be managed to work efficiently. You will need to manage your portfolio to gain the most from it. You see, you need to constantly ensure that it is kept in balance. Now I'm not talking about geographic spread, but rather a balance between the different types of property deals that will produce your income stream."

Sarah was beginning to look a little puzzled and shot a quick glance at her husband. He smiled reassuringly back. She knew that meant she needn't worry; he understood.

"Aim to do one quick cash deal to get you up and running," the Coach continued. "Then, using the proceeds, buy a positive cashflow property, followed by another quick cash deal, to help finance your next positive cashflow deal. Keep doing this until you have sufficient positive cashlow deals in place to make the payments on a negatively geared (capital growth) property and purchase one."

Brian murmured to himself, as if he should have guessed how this would work.

"An alternative strategy to accumulate your positive cashflow property is to buy each one at a solid discount and renovate, creating immediate equity that becomes your deposit to roll into the next property like we discussed last week, and continue this process over and over again."

"You may only need one quick cash deal to fund your purchases, or in some cases, like yourselves, you already have equity and good incomes, so you probably won't need many of them at all."

Sarah was, as always, writing quickly.

"People often think you can't purchase property at a discount, but frankly that's rubbish. What they mean is *they* can't purchase property at a discount. With the right skills and training, anyone can do it. After following this concept, a beginner investor should now have four positive cashflow properties and one that is negatively geared. Consider them as an entity. They become a stand-alone property investment entity or unit."

"What do you mean by this, Coach?" Sarah asked a little sheepishly.

"Think of the four or five positive cashflow properties and the one negatively geared property as separate pieces that work in unison to produce the results you are after. They all rely on each other to deliver the required results."

Sarah nodded and made a few more notes but still looked puzzled.

"Think about this simple example. Let's say you bought four $100,000 properties that were cashflow positive, then to balance your portfolio you would probably buy a $400,000 capital growth property. The income from the four positive properties would cover the loss on the negative property."

"That way our borrowing capacity is still good," added Brian.

"Also, many countries have capital gains tax or a tax on trading property that does not apply to long-term property investments. Because of this you may want to treat your quick cash deals as a separate business rather than a part of your Property Wealth Wheel because there are no tax advantages in doing so. Check with your accountant about this first."

"Careful planning with a good real estate accountant can save you thousands of dollars. It's very costly having to reconfigure your property portfolio because you didn't do your homework and purchased real estate in the wrong entities. If I had one piece of crucial advice for new property investors, it would be to start as you mean to continue and take time out to set up the correct structure with your lawyers and accountants from day one."

Brian looked up and asked how long it takes, on average, to set up such a wheel.

"It is easily possible to establish a complete Property Wealth Wheel in your first year if you start with solid equity and a good income, but others may take 10 years or more to get one completed. It's really up to you," the Coach replied.

"Each wheel will then spin off another wheel every several years, purely on the equity it will contain as the values grow. It's important to remember not to rush out and start buying. You will be excited and eager to get some runs on the board, but you must work according to your plan. This is where your rules come in. Keep reminding yourself of them and what your ultimate outcome is. Sometimes it's better to take a little longer to get your first deal and start with a great one rather than an okay one."

The Coach reached for his glass of water and took a long drink. Then he continued.

"Let's assume you have now done all this and you are quite comfortable about how you are going to go about setting up your first Property Wealth Wheel. The first thing you will be looking for is a quick cash deal or a discounted deal if you want to follow the second part of the strategy. You'll begin by doing all the things property buyers do. You'll study the real estate pages in your local newspaper, look in the windows of Realtor's offices, visit their Web sites, speak to agents, and visit open houses. The more effort here, the better the result.

"Now remember, it's a quick cash deal you are after. What happens if you come across a great deal—a real beauty that represents great value? Only trouble is, it's a positive cashflow house and that's outside your investing rules. What should you do? Pass up a once-in-a-lifetime deal, or buy while the going's good?"

He looked at Sarah for the answer.

"You walk away and keep looking," she replied.

"That's right. Don't let your ego, emotions, or enthusiasm distract you from your game plan. You must stick to the rules and look for a quick cash deal. If you don't, you're well on your way to becoming an ordinary property owner all over again. Now I know this isn't easy, but if it were, everyone would be doing it, and succeeding."

The value of having a good set of rules suddenly dawned on Brian. He had seen the light.

"Another thing to bear in mind is that, with quick cash deals, it's all about stock turnover. You see, you have to remember you need to treat this game as you would a business. And business is all about stock turnover. You can buy, renovate, and sell a property in six months (assuming you take a month to find a property, a month for the deal to settle, another month to renovate, then a month to resell it and a month for that sale to settle). If you could speed up this process to allow you to do three such deals a year instead of two, it'll make the world of difference. Time is money."

Brian knew the Coach was talking sense. It was, after all, a sound business principle that he was only too well aware of, but he also knew he needed to learn and his first deal would take a little more time.

"But don't cut corners. I never put a property back on the market until the renovation is complete. This is because potential buyers may still remember it as it was before you bought it and dismiss it without a second look. Remember, they chose not to buy it then, so they'll have preconceived ideas about what could, and what couldn't, be done with it.

"You see, where I make my money is by changing the property from what it was then to what it is now. That's how I can justify a higher price. It's not often you can buy something, slap on a coat of paint and cut the lawn, then resell it for a vastly increased price. I will generally change the use of the property, change its appearance, or change its functionality. And I've often resold that very same property back to either the previous vendor or a buyer who had seen it prerenovation, and got my price, because they didn't see what I saw in it to start with."

"Coach, is there a reason it's four positives to one negative?" Sarah changed the subject just a little.

"Great point. As you become wealthier you'll really want more and more capital growth deals, but at the beginning you need to manage borrowing capacity, so yes at the start the four to one ratio is vital for income purposes. As you create more wealth and more income, it gradually changes to three positive to two negatives and so on."

The Coach gave them their homework of finding at least three positive cashflow suburbs or towns they could start investing in and three capital growth suburbs as well. They knew they would be busy during the next week.

Wealth Wheel—
The Property Wealth Wheel is a simple concept.
It consists of just three components: negatively geared deals, positive cashflow deals, and a funding source that can be either quick cash deals in a property boom or my business or job at other times. The Wealth Wheel changes its portfolio balance as I become wealthier.

"It's now time to think about some basic concepts that should underpin your plan of action," the Coach commented at the beginning of their next session. "You see, I believe you need to understand whether you will be taking a long-term or short-term view regarding your property purchases. Now there will obviously be times when you will most definitely be buying short term, like in a quick cash situation, but you need to remember that it is futile attempting this in a flat market."

The Coach allowed Sarah to catch up with her notes before continuing.

"This is because it is obviously more difficult to sell in a slow market, isn't it? And, most of the time, that is around 7 out of every 10 years the property market is flat, sideways, or even negative."

Both Brian and Sarah nodded in agreement. It stood to reason that in a slow market there would be fewer buyers than sellers and therefore buyers would have the upper hand. They would be calling the shots and this would generally mean the seller would achieve a lower price. This, of course, is not the goal of the quick cash sale.

"You also need to know what you are doing because if you don't, you could make an expensive mistake. Short-term deals must be thought of very much as business decisions; there must be sound reasons for doing so. And, of course, business decisions usually involve an element of risk, don't they?"

Again both Brian and Sarah nodded.

"It is always safer and wiser to take a long-term view when it comes to investing in real estate. Think of it this way: Would my grandchildren like the fact that I bought this property and left it to them in 50 to 60 years?"

Brian laughed as he thought of how short term his investment thinking had really been, wondering if he could turn a profit in 12 months or two years.

Short Term versus Long Term—
Short-term property investing should be called trading
and be thought of more as a business than investing.
Short-term investing should only ever be attempted by
people with solid knowledge and in a real estate boom.
Long-term investing is the safer, more intelligent, and
generally better returning option.

"Another basic concept I want to discuss now is the whole nasty area of overcommitting. See, this is something that so many inexperienced real estate investors do. It's got to be one of the biggest traps that await the uninitiated."

Brian had always been aware of this; it was probably the one main reason he hadn't become a property investor sooner. He had seen many of his friends make this mistake over the years and he knew he was a sucker when it came to buying. He had always jumped in and gotten swept away with all the emotion. He thought back to his foray into the boat world recently. He shuddered at what the result of that might have been if he had committed to a cruiser instead of investing.

"This is one of the most compelling reasons to not only having a good set of rules before you start," the Coach continued, "but it is an excellent reason for following them."

He paused to let that sink in.

"Stick to your rules and you will never go wrong. You won't be blinded by a great deal that comes your way that doesn't quite fit with what you are after."

It had been another short but huge session and both Brian and Sarah were feeling ready for a break. They weren't used to being so mentally stimulated, especially as it had been not only the weekly coaching sessions but the homework as well. But because they knew it was something that would result in a meaningful improvement of their entire lifestyle, they didn't mind in the least.

Brian kept thinking about a profound saying he had read years before: *The only difference between you now and the you in five years' time is the books you read, the people you meet, and the actions you take.* He had never forgotten this and now he really understood its true meaning.

Overcommitting—
Overcommiting is the biggest killer of investors in property—people who can't say *no* to a deal. Although this is a real danger, if I stick to my rules and do my numbers, I will never overcommit myself or my resources.

Part 3

▌Buy Land Value, Not Houses

The Coach had mentioned that the next few sessions would be concentrated on some of the fundamentals which would greatly assist them when it came to refining their rules. He promised that these fundamentals would help them avoid making some of the basic mistakes that so many small-time investors do.

"If you understand some of the fundamentals," the Coach began, "it will become clear in your own minds just what the attraction of investing in real estate is, compared to say, the stock market."

Brian loved this stuff. Not only did he find it stimulating, but it gave him direction.

"The real attraction of the real estate market is land. Land is a commodity that will not grow on a tree as they say, so it should keep on appreciating. So let's look at this in a little detail. What parts of a city have the most valuable land, land that should grow faster in value than anywhere else?" the Coach asked.

"Well, the inner city would be a start, and land on the water," Brian started.

"And land with views, or near parks and forests, or even in prestigious suburbs," added Sarah.

"Great," said the Coach. "All the higher capital growth areas. Remember that any city that has water nearby will have higher growth between the city and the water than any other area. Now, that brings us to our next point: how will you work out what the land value is in any suburb?"

"You can check into local land sales," blurted Brian.

"And, if there are no sales, like in an old-money suburb?" the Coach questioned.

"Maybe local land taxes or even ask a realtor," Sarah added thoughtfully.

"Good stuff; so central to all of this is what main point?

"That the land is where the value is, Coach," Sarah continued.

"And, that we should know the land value before making an offer, Coach," Brian replied.

The Coach's notes explained it simply.

Land Up—
They're not making any more land. Investing in property
is all about owning a piece of dirt with a building that
pays for the land under it. Over time, it's the land
value that will make me the most money.

"Now if the land goes up in value and ultimately the increase in value is what creates your wealth, what is the house or building for?" the Coach asked.

"To pay for it along the way," Brian replied. "Without a house you have nothing to rent, and nothing to create income or even tax deductions."

The Coach smiled. His students were learning fast.

"That's one of the main reasons I prefer to invest in houses rather than condos, units, and bare land," he continued. "See, it's fine when the building is new, but as time goes by—and we are talking about a long-term investment here—the building deteriorates. It requires maintenance and upgrading. All this costs money. The intrinsic value of the building will diminish over time. That's why even most governments allow you to depreciate it over the length of its life when it comes to tax.

"Some governments say the building will last only 25 years, others depreciate it over 40 years, so be clear that the building will need refurbishment every 10 to 12 years and replacement at some stage in the future."

"And I guess you can always build new buildings, whereas with land, once it's taken, it's taken. You simply can't get any more," Sarah commented.

"That's absolutely right, Sarah. It's all a question of supply and demand, isn't it?

"So, what other important point does this bring up for us to remember when we develop our rules?" asked the Coach, trying to see if his students were really catching on.

Both Brian and Sarah looked at each other and then back to the Coach. It was Brian who spoke up first. "Bigger lots will be worth more in the future, so if you can buy the same size house on a bigger lot, then you should do that."

"Excellent thinking, but there is an even more important point." The Coach was now smiling as he spoke. "Are there areas in your city and most other major cities you know of where once it was all houses but now it's full of high rises or apartment blocks?"

"A lot, Coach." Brian started to nod. "So if we buy something now that we will own for a long time, we could even move to building more than one rentable house or condo on our current land."

"This is getting easier; you guys are catching on fast." The Coach was now really grinning and both Brian and Sarah smiled with pride.

Building Down—
Buildings deteriorate over time, so it's only to
be expected that they will lose value.
Most governments in the world agree by allowing us to
depreciate the property over its life.

"Let's go on to the next note I've given you. It's still true that location is everything in real estate. A good address has always been desirable from buyers' points of view. They will pay a premium just to be living in the right location. This could be because of social considerations as much as for factors such as convenience to major amenities, the city, schools and sporting facilities, or transportation. And, of course, aesthetic considerations such as the view, proximity to the beach or rivers, and the like have a major impact on the value of a good location."

Sarah was shuffling in her chair, marshalling her thoughts before speaking.

"But these are the very properties that are the most expensive, Coach," she said. "That's why most of us can't afford them."

"True. But a good location will always remain a good location, won't it? That's why I am always attracted to a property if it happens to be the worst house on the best street. If you can find one of these, it will be the cheapest entry you'll ever get to a desirable neighborhood. These are great buys and something to be on the lookout for."

The Coach continued as if he were just thinking aloud: "And, the exact opposite is a really big mistake. People buy the biggest and best house on the worst street or in the worst neighborhood. This is crazy, because you have to remember that the land has the value, not the building. If you think the house you're looking at is the best on the street, run away, go for the worst on the street, and either renovate or just tidy it up."

Both Brian and Sarah had already read the Coach's note.

Worst House, Best Street—
Because the name of the game has always been about
location, location, location, owning the worst house on
the best street is what will make me money. That also goes
for the worst street in the best neighborhood, etc.

"So how do we pick the highest growth areas, Coach?" Brian asked. "I mean, looking at the asking prices may be an indication but if this were the case, then surely we wouldn't be able to invest in such areas until we had built up good reserves of cash to get us started."

"Price may be a consequence of a property's being situated in a high growth area, but on its own it isn't an indicator," the Coach replied. He picked up a folder on his desk, opened it, and withdrew two sheets of paper, which he handed to Brian and Sarah.

"Here are some good indicators of high growth areas. Have a good look at them and be guided by them."

The Coach busies himself with some more paperwork while they read.

City Center

Properties close to the city center are always in demand, as people like to live close to work and their social scene.

Water

People love living on the water, close to the water, and where they can see the water. Properties between the city center and the water usually have a higher level of demand.

Hills

Scenery and breezes are hard to beat; properties close to or in the hills score on both counts.

Old Money

Older, well-established residential areas usually attract premium prices and appreciate well over time. As people become wealthier they want to move to these suburbs, as generally the schools and other amenities are better, creating extra demand.

High Growth Usually Equals Low Cashflow

You generally can't have it both ways; high growth properties will usually provide great returns in the long run but you can't usually expect to receive a good cashflow at the same time.

High-Growth Areas—
If it's high growth I am after, then I need to
look for the well-known identifiers where capital
growth is created by extra demand.

"The other general type of area you can invest in is the lower-growth, high-cashflow areas," the Coach continued.

"Think of these properties as your cash cows. They may not appreciate greatly in the short term but they will produce a good income stream and solid growth over the long term. You would also buy these because they make it feasible for you to cover the ongoing cost of investing in a property in a high-growth area."

Again, he passed two sheets of paper from a folder on his desk as he spoke.

"Once again, study this sheet well and take it into account when establishing your rules. It provides excellent indicators of where to look to find low-growth areas."

Brian slid his sheet into his folder, preferring to go over it later at home. Sarah was still taking notes but did glance at it to clarify a point she wanted to highlight.

Mid to Outer Suburbs

The further from the city center, the cheaper a property usually becomes as the land value decreases. As the land is worth less but it still costs the same to build the house, rental returns generally get better.

Smaller Towns

Properties in smaller towns are generally more affordable but have higher rents because demand for them is less and land costs less, but the risk of fewer people renting means you have to charge higher rents. Remember the building costs about the same so rent and yields should be better by comparison.

Lower Socioeconomic Class

Properties in working class suburbs are generally in more demand as rentals than they are for people wanting to own, so the rental yields are often greater.

Low Growth Usually Equals High Cashflow

You can usually get great cashflow from properties that have limited middle-term growth prospects; they usually are good cashflow renters.

**Low-Growth Areas—
Lower growth usually means higher cashflow,
so if it's positive cashflow I'm after, then I need to look for
the well-known identifiers where rental yields are higher.**

"It helps if you understand what part of the property growth cycle you are in at any point in time," the Coach continued.

"You see, property usually grows in cycles. They used to call it the seven-year cycle, but times have changed and so have the timings of the cycles." The Coach looked towards the ceiling as he thought about how the cycles had built his wealth.

"Very simply put, there are indicators as to where you are in the cycle of boom and bust, or, as I like to refer to it, the seasons of property investment.

"For example, summer is when we have boom times, values are climbing, there are lots of buyers, and everyone is extremely happy. People think the summer will never end, but, of course, it always does, and some are left out in the cold.

"Then, of course, comes fall, or autumn as they call it in some parts of the world, where prices start to stagnate and then fall as demand drops off and everyone starts to hibernate for the winter, stocking up and not buying. And only those who literally have to sell do so.

"As winter sets in, people wonder if the cold will ever go away, realtors are making no money, the market isn't moving at all, and prices are generally sideways on low volumes, meaning that very few people are selling.

"Then spring sets in and as with nature, some trees bud first, while others wait until it's truly summer before they invest and notice the new season.

"The market follows this cycle with regularity and most people can easily identify the market. The important thing is to act on what you know."

"So how do you know what phase of the cycle we are in, Coach?" Sarah asked.

"This is where knowing your market comes in, Sarah. By having a good handle of prices in your chosen market, you will know when they begin to move up or down. And by watching the ads on a weekly basis, you will also get a very good idea of when there is a glut of property or even rentals on the market or when there is a shortage."

She was nodding as she took notes.

"And by visiting open houses, you will be able to gauge whether there are many buyers on the market or not. Talking to the agents also tells you much. And don't forget to read the papers continuously. By the time the papers say there is a boom, it's probably already too late to make your move and buy great bargains. Remember, the papers are always a little behind true market movements, and so are bank valuations.

"Just remember to watch every indicator, like interest rates. As they drop we move into spring and as they climb here comes fall."

The Coach had both Brian and Sarah turn to their next notes.

> Traditional Growth Cycle—
> Like everything else, real estate grows in cycles.
> By understanding and monitoring its growth cycle,
> I can maximize my returns. Usually a few years of high
> growth are followed by some downward movement and
> then several more years sideways before another boom.
> When you see statistics telling you property values
> grow at around 10 percent a year, remember that
> growth doesn't happen every year; these numbers
> are most often quoted as an average.

"So, what happens if you missed spring and it was early summer before you thought you should really start investing?" the Coach questioned Brian directly.

"Not sure, Coach. Maybe get a little further out from the city," he answered.

"If you happen to be in the market once it has started to move upward, don't be alarmed; all is not lost. You can still make excellent buys if you can identify a pocket or area that hasn't begun to climb yet. These are usually situated between two suburbs that have begun to rocket. So the key is to have your finger on the pulse and to be proactive."

Sarah looked up sharply and said, "Another good reason to make sure we stay well informed, Coach. It is becoming really clear to me the importance of becoming as knowledgeable as possible about our market."

"That's right, Sarah. I can't stress this enough. Remember what I said about risk equaling a lack of knowledge? The less you know about the market, the riskier it becomes. And when you consider that you are playing for huge stakes here, why wouldn't you do whatever it takes to ensure your investment is as safe as possible?

"Also, remember this very important point, that you might have two suburbs near highways or rail lines that have moved up in value, but it may be that the one suburb in the middle hasn't gone up in value yet. Keep looking and you'll find little pockets that have not risen in value like the areas around them. These can be great opportunities.

Brian knew the Coach was talking sense. It was much like investing in the stock market. Professional traders spent a considerable amount of time and money making sure their market intelligence was as good as possible. Casual investors didn't—or couldn't for whatever reason—and this is why their investments were never as sure as those of the professionals. It stood to reason, he thought to himself as he completed his notes. He wouldn't fall into the same trap.

Undervalued Pockets—
When the market moves, it usually does so in stages.
If I can locate undervalued pockets in between
two suburbs or areas that have already grown,
I can make great investment returns.

"Remember what I said about location?"

Both Brian and Sarah nodded. They knew that, in real estate, this was what it was all about.

"Most people want convenience," the Coach continued.

"That usually means living close to the amenities they use or value most. And that includes work, because getting to and from one's place of work is a major expense. Just ask anyone who lives one or two hours away from the office!"

Brian understood the principle and wondered where the Coach was headed.

"So when it comes to monitoring your marketplace, the thing to do is watch price movements in the inner city areas because they are usually the first to move. The movement here has a ripple effect on the rest of the market because prices in adjacent suburbs will be next to move. This is because those people who really want to live in the inner city suddenly find they can no longer afford to buy there because of price rises. So they go to the next closest suburbs to look for accommodation, causing demand there. This causes the prices there to rise. Those who can't afford these suburbs any longer move a little further out and so the price rise ripples further and further out."

Brian was excited by what he was hearing.

"So if we were able to monitor this ripple effect, Coach, we'd be able to buy in a suburb that was just ahead of the price rise and then sell when the suburb took off."

"See how knowledge helps reduce risk?" the Coach laughed.

"One other way this applies," the Coach added. "Usually bigger cities in a state or country move in price first followed by smaller cities based on their size until eventually the smallest towns furthest from any large cities move. It's a great way to know what city or town to go to next."

City Center Out—
Usually demand is created on the city center,
pushing its prices up first and gradually moving out
to the suburbs as people need to move further out
to afford what they want. Watching the prices move,
from the city center out, can assist me in planning
which areas to target before they begin to move.

"Remember when we were discussing the fact that you buy property either for its capital growth potential or for the rental returns it brings?" the Coach asked.

"Yes, I certainly do," Brian replied, and waited to see where this was headed.

"And remember that I mentioned you buy for one or the other reason and not both?"

Brian nodded.

"Well, this would imply that the two were unconnected, wouldn't it?" he continued.

This time it was Sarah who agreed.

"Wrong. See, they are connected in that the one affects the other. When property prices rise, there is a lag before rents rise. This makes rents seem very reasonable compared to house prices. This is usually because tenants are on lease agreements which only permit rentals to rise periodically. But eventually rents do catch up and will eventually be in proportion to the price of the house."

"Will rents ever exceed the proportional value of the house, Coach?" Brian asked.

"Good question. And, yes they will, but this will in turn put upward pressure on prices, causing the cycle to commence all over again. It's like a seesaw."

Once again, Brian felt he had achieved much during the session. And tiring as it was, he relished the thought that he had direction in his life once more. It was almost as if he had been revitalized.

He had tried to remain as focused as possible during the session so that he would retain as much information as possible; he instinctively knew this would stand him in good stead when the time came for him to get out in the marketplace and begin the hunt for their first investment property.

Cashflow versus Growth Seesaw—
When a property boom pushes prices up, the rentals
seem low; they eventually catch up and surpass values as a
percentage and thus values grow, and so on. These two
factors are always trying to balance but usually just keep
creating more growth as demand kicks in.

Part 4

▌Buy Residential Real Estate

The weekly coaching sessions had now become part of Brian's and Sarah's routine. And they had become passionate about being in a learning mode once more. After all, they had first met as carefree students all those years ago when life seemed so much more fun.

They had always talked often about their days at school and university together; they had a really good circle of friends back then too. Somehow life had never quite been the same once the responsibilities of marriage, a young family, and their careers began to take over.

But now things were somehow different. They felt almost as if they had traveled back in time and become two inseparable youngsters all over again. Sarah wondered if this was what reincarnation was all about.

"Everyone needs to live somewhere," the Coach said as he kicked off the weekly session. "If you invest in the mid to low property price range, there will almost always be people wanting to rent."

Brian nodded in agreement; this was, after all, the very reason most people were attracted to the real estate market, he thought. Sarah opened her notebook and prepared to begin writing.

"I very seldom buy a high-priced single-dwelling property in a prime location for rental return," the Coach continued.

"I buy properties in that higher price range for capital growth. If there happens to be a tenant paying top dollar, all well and good, but if they're only paying a lower rental, I don't care. My higher rental income comes from properties in the mid to low price range. That's where the cashflow is. These properties are always in demand and they're always rented out. If you have a balanced property portfolio, then your lower-priced properties will pay for your higher-priced ones. The only time I buy cashflow properties in the higher price range is when the figures look very, very good or I buy blocks of units or multiple income properties on one site."

Brian looked up and said, "I guess supply and demand is what it is all about."

The Coach nodded.

"Understanding supply and demand factors makes life very easy. And what I like about it is that as a property owner, I get to choose. I choose so that things suit me. Let me explain what I mean by this."

Sarah prepared to take notes.

"Owning rental property is a fairly predictable business. You can spot the trends: For example, people tend to get transferred or move at Christmas time. Keeping these trends in mind, you can choose when you buy, where you buy, and when and where to sell."

Sarah's pen was working overtime.

"So, simply put then, Coach, we have to look at where people want to move to as well as where they are now," Sarah spoke as she wrote.

"Great thinking, Sarah."

Demand and Supply—
Whether it is job growth, migration rates,
infrastructure growth, or higher prices pushing people
further out from the city center, rental rates grow
with supply and demand, as do property prices.

"Unlike most rental property owners, I don't always operate on the basis of signing a six-month or yearly lease or rental agreement with my tenants," the Coach began.

Sarah looked surprised.

"What do you mean, Coach? Surely that's the way it is done? If you choose not to 'play by the rules,' then what do you do?"

"I play by my rules," the Coach responded.

"See, I work on the principle that the properties become vacant in early January each year. So in some cases the lease or rental agreement would be for nine months, in others for 22 months, depending when it was signed. Now most times I will use the normal timing, but not if all my properties in that area are on the same time frame."

"Oh, I get it. You still do play by the rules; it's just that you often amend them to suit you."

"That's right, Sarah. I treat this like a business. It has to deliver me the returns I wanted when I bought. Remember, it's all about the numbers. But there's more than just the length of the lease when it comes to ensuring your numbers stack up. You need to ensure that your property is occupied and producing you a rental income for as much of the year as possible."

This time it was Brian who was taking the notes.

"So to do this, I also never let a property become vacant on a Saturday because then it would take me a day or two to get it cleaned and readvertised, with usually the earliest prospect of reletting it being the following Saturday. That way I lose a whole week's rent. If I choose to let it become vacant on Wednesday, I can get it cleaned and readvertised within a day or so, allowing me to rent it out that same Saturday, a day that also suits most people wanting to move.

"One of the keys to choosing good property or rental managers is how well they move people out and then in. The best in the industry can get one group out on a Saturday morning and another in that afternoon."

Sarah remembered back to the days they rented and now understood why they had to move out so early on Saturday.

"This way I only have the place unoccupied for a few hours, and I've lost no rental income at all. It's a small detail, but when you're renting out many properties like I do, it all adds up to many tens of thousands of dollars.

"So, here's a question. Why do some properties remain vacant for a long period of time?" the Coach questioned the couple.

"Oh, I remember this one, Coach, they either need cleaning up or repairing," Brian jumped in over Sarah.

"And, Sarah, do you remember the other main reasons?" The Coach made sure Sarah had a chance to speak.

"Sure do, Coach. It's probably overpriced and the owners for some strange reason want to hold out for their price instead of knocking $10 to $15 a week from the rental price, or the other is that they bought a property in an area with no rental demand."

"Great stuff, team. By the way, why do I always refer to rental income in weekly terms and not monthly?" the Coach again asked to see if they were thinking.

Both Brian and Sarah had no idea and shrugged.

"Let me show you: First it's about moving people in and out easily and second and more importantly, weekly rental is 52 weeks whereas monthly rental is often miscalculated into 12 × 4, which equals 48 weeks only."

"Wow, Coach, that's 4 weeks' rent missed a year," spouted Brian.

"Yes, miscalculations can cost you a lot of money. If you do want it monthly, be sure to work it out on a daily rate," the Coach handed them his notes as he spoke.

Vacancy Rates—
I can manage my vacancies far better in residential than in other types of property. As long as my property is clean, tidy, and in good condition, I'll usually get a tenant. If not, I can usually drop $5 or $10 a week to get it rented.

"It amazes me that people think owning a lot of property is risky," the Coach continued. "The reality is the more properties you own, the less risk you face financially. It's a pretty good reason for being a serious property investor who gets some runs on the board rather than someone who just dabbles with one or two properties."

For once, both Brian and Sarah were speechless.

"In real estate, everything is insurable. Well, almost everything. The only thing that isn't is a planned vacancy. But as with everything, you need to approach it with the right attitude if you want to avoid any nasty surprises."

Brian nodded.

"When owning rental property, you might not need to make an insurance claim right away. It may be that you only need to claim in a year's time for some damages suffered during the first year's tenancy. It may be only when your first tenant moves out and you are preparing the house for the next tenant that you discover something that necessitates a claim. It may be that in the last month of your current insurance policy that you need to claim for fire or storm damage. You pay your premiums based on values in 12 months' time. For this reason, it's better to overinsure than to underinsure."

Brian knew this to be a wise policy. He had experienced incidents at work where they were sorry they hadn't been overinsured.

"You also need to bear in mind that most insurance policies include a 'subject to average' clause. This means if you have underinsured by 50 percent, they will only pay out 50 percent of your claim. These are the rules of the game, and if you play, you must play by the rules. You must understand the rules, and if you play by them, at least you'll get paid when you make a claim. And believe me, the time will come when you will make a claim."

"Are there other forms of insurance we need to know about, Coach?" Brian asked.

"Yes, there certainly are. In most countries banks will insist you have mortgage insurance if you have borrowed more than 80 percent of the purchase price of a property. Then there's home and contents or chattels insurance that is well worth taking out."

Brian was listening intently while Sarah jotted down the details.

"Don't take out a private household policy on a rental property. Rather take out a landlord's policy, as this generally includes some contents insurance at the base rate to cover carpets, curtains, stove, light fixtures, and things like that. Make sure the policy also includes property owner's liability, not just public liability. Make sure you have this because if you don't, it's the sort of thing that can leave you broke."

This was something that had been troubling Brian, so he was pleased to hear that there was a way around it.

"You should also consider policies that cover debt recovery, legal bills, and tenant damage. When you buy a rental property, it's important to ensure that you get a landlord's protection policy or something similar. This is a very good product, as it includes checks on prospective tenants to make sure they're good tenants, checks of the tenant black list, and credit checks in general. If a tenant breaks a lease, lost rent is covered, and repairs up to an amount set on your policy are paid if the tenant does any damage to the property. Downtime of up to 52 weeks is also covered during the period the house is being repaired, and the cost of legal bills incurred and debt recovery costs are also included. This is a reasonable policy for the price, and it guarantees your income all the time."

He paused and drank from the glass on his desk.

"Another policy to consider is a personal accident or sickness income protection policy. Your income is, after all, your greatest asset. Protect it. And don't forget to include a mortgage payout clause in your policy.

"When you are ready to go deeper into this topic, I would suggest you contact a reputable registered insurance broker. Just remember to pay your premiums on time and to insure for too much, not too little."

"I have saved a packet of money by using one insurance broker to handle the insurance for all my properties and having all the policies come up for renewal at the same time. This enables the broker to negotiate a discounted bulk insurance package that saves me thousands each year. It is also a whole lot easier to have one bulk insurance renewal each year than policies coming up for renewal each week or month."

> Insurance—
> Entrusting my investment property to strangers
> can be a risk; I need to be almost overinsured to cover
> any eventuality. The great thing about property is
> that almost everything is insurable.

Sarah completed her note-taking, leaned back in her chair, stretched noisily, and said, "I guess it stands to reason, Coach, that demand for rental properties will have an effect on the prices of houses in general."

She thought this to be a rather good question and was pleased with herself. She didn't want the Coach to think of her as an "ordinary" person. She had always thought she had more potential than she had made use of. Life can be cruel in this regard, she thought.

"That's very astute of you, Sarah. Well done. And yes, this is the great thing about being a property investor. Not only do you earn an income from the rents your properties generate; your tenants help you pay off your asset as well. And if that weren't good enough, the properties invariably appreciate as time goes by, so you also stand to make a capital gain at the end of the day.

"What's more," the Coach kept pushing on, "You control the growth of the entire asset with only a small portion of cash invested. With only $20,000 in cash you receive the growth of a $100,000 asset."

They had covered a whole lot more than they had expected before the coaching session began. Brian was more than delighted, and Sarah felt that she was smarter than she had sometimes believed. This session had done wonders for her self-esteem and for that alone she was more than grateful.

But they were not yet through. The Coach showed no signs of finishing.

> People Pay for My Asset—
> Real estate is all about leverage; I control a growth asset
> and have someone else pay a percentage of my holding
> costs as it grows.

Brian pondered what he had just heard. Taking a moment to marshal his thoughts, he said: "We are part of a growing population, aren't we, Coach? And that means now is the right time to start investing."

"Of course, this is in essence what it's all about," the Coach responded. "We are providing housing, at a profit, for the bulk of the population. And the population just keeps getting bigger, doesn't it? Not only that, but a higher percentage of them are now renting. Of course, some areas are better than others when it comes to rental demand, so do your homework. It's not difficult; it just takes some common sense and a little effort."

Brian nodded as he scribbled down a few notes of his own.

"As I've mentioned before, statistics covering the last three decades around the world show that over this period the number of renters has grown from around 20 percent to around 30 percent. This seems to be a global trend."

He paused to let the significance of what he had just said sink in.

"Remember what this means: There has been an unbelievable demand for new rental properties, and the vast majority of them are supplied by private investors like you and me!"

Providing Accommodation—
People have to live somewhere. As a landlord and
investor, I provide an absolute must for the community—
accommodation. Most governments do not want to and
cannot afford to provide enough rental housing.

"Now I'd like you to do this little exercise before our next meeting," the Coach said as he made a note of their next coaching session in his appointment book.

"Consider it part of your research. Imagine you are looking to rent a house for yourself to live in. Choose the area you would prefer and get out and have a look at what's available. What will you find? I'm sure you'll be surprised at how difficult it is to find a decent place that you'd be happy to live in. Many landlords seem to think anything will do."

Sarah smiled. This was the type of exercise she liked doing. Practical stuff.

"It's not difficult to place yourself in an enviable position on the rental market just by presenting your property in a decent manner. With only a little effort and common sense, you'll have tenants clamoring after your property. By doing the right thing as a landlord, you should never have to worry about poor occupancy rates."

"Pretend you're an average family with an average income and just see what's available."

Average Family—
Three or four bedrooms and two bathrooms
with a driveway or garage; my ideal target market
is the average family. I must make sure my
investment properties meet the needs of the
average family in the area where I'm investing.

"There is one more topic I want to quickly open up today," the Coach said. "And that's financing."

Brian cleared his throat and said: "Or getting into debt."

He had become more conscious of the need to pay off all his debts well before the time came for him to retire.

"Getting into debt isn't always a bad thing, Brian," the Coach replied.

"Of course, it makes a huge difference whether the debt you're about to take on is good debt or bad debt. There's a big difference between these two. Let me explain."

Sarah flipped over to a clean page in her notebook.

"Good debt is that which makes you money. It's used to buy assets. It's something someone else pays for on your behalf. Bad debt, on the other hand, is something you have to pay for. It's consumer debt. You pay for it with your after-tax money. Unfortunately, this is the type of debt most people accumulate."

"Can you give us a few examples?" Sarah asked.

"Sure. Cars and houses can be good debt. But things like cameras, computers, clothes, vacations, and other toys are bad debt. I'll never, ever owe money on any of them. You see, the day you buy them, they're worth virtually nothing. Technology is already obsolete the day you buy. And if you sold it a month after you bought, you'd only get back a fraction of the price you paid."

Sarah nodded as she wrote.

"But with real estate, it's different," the Coach continued.

"The banks are lining up to provide you and me with money to buy good properties. But that doesn't mean they hand out the money to just anyone. There are certain criteria they look at. You still do need to satisfy certain requirements. To put it simply, there are three attributes you'll need if you want to borrow money. They are strength of income, strength of assets, and strength of nerves."

Brian smiled.

"When you are considering borrowing, just remember valuations are one thing, but serviceability is still a bank's main concern. Their bottom line is ensuring that they minimize their risks. It's not so much about how much you can borrow; it's rather about how much you can service, or pay back, that's important here."

"So we need to manage ourselves well," Sarah muttered, as if to herself.

"That's right, Sarah. You need to manage your Loan to Valuation Ratio, or what we call LVR, as well as your finance options to make sure you can keep growing your wealth."

She looked up from her notes a little confused and asked: "What is a Loan to Valuation Ratio, Coach?"

"It's a calculation that determines how much money the lender will loan you against your security. For example, if your bank sets the LVR for a property at 70%, they will lend you $140,000 to buy a $200,000 property. So by investing $60,000 of your own money you could end up with a property worth at least $200,000. I say 'at least' because if you buy well, the property should be worth a whole lot more."

As they drove home, Brian suddenly felt exhausted. The intensity of the session was beginning to take effect. Yet he found it strangely stimulating.

Finance—
Bankers and financiers are lining up to help me buy more properties. I need to manage my LVR and my finance options to make sure I can keep growing my wealth.

Part 5

∎ Buy, Reno, Redraw

Sarah knew the time was close. She felt it in her bones.

Brian could feel it too. And the anticipation was beginning to show.

"I can't believe we are getting close to the time when we are going to get out there and begin buying properties," she said as they climbed into their car and made their way to the Coach's office for their weekly session.

"I'm really excited, but at the same time a little nervous. I mean, are we really ready for this yet?"

Brian knew exactly how she felt.

"What worries me is not knowing whether we are actually getting ourselves into something that is way beyond us."

Sarah nodded. "Yes," she agreed. "It worries me that we will be making a huge mistake financially. It's not as if we are well off or anything. We can't afford to make a mistake at this stage of our lives."

This had been troubling Brian too as the weeks had progressed. Until now he had pushed the thought from his mind whenever it surfaced because he knew it would bring on the dreaded stomach pains. Yet deep down he knew they were on the right track. His instinct told him so.

"I have this gut feeling that we need to pursue it, Sarah. It's really a case of now or never. And in any case, what's the worst that can happen?"

"I suppose you are right," she replied. "I do trust and believe in what the Coach has been showing us. I guess I'm just a little nervous because we have never done anything like this in the past."

Brian parked the car outside the Coach's office and was still deep in thought as they climbed out and made their way to the front door. It did vaguely cross his mind that he could hardly recall the journey there.

"Hello, folks," the Coach said on opening the door. "Come on in; we have a lot to get through today."

He led them through to his office and beckoned them to their chairs.

"We are now going to discuss how to go about buying your first, and subsequent, investment properties."

Sarah felt her heartbeat speed up.

"But remember, when you get out there with real estate agents, they are acting on behalf of the seller and not you. They will be trying every trick in the book to get you to make an offer—and a good one at that."

"Good from the seller's point of view," Brian added.

"That's absolutely right. And that's why it's vitally important to understand how this game works, and to stick to your rules and the rules of the game."

Brian looked at Sarah and smiled. The significance of what they had already discussed during the previous few coaching sessions was beginning to sink in.

How to Buy—
Buying an investment property is about
evaluation and doing my homework. I need to understand
the process to be followed when buying my investment
property; play the game and follow the rules for a better
chance of scoring well.

"Negotiating the deal is the most important activity in real estate because it's where you make your immediate equity or the first form of money you make," the Coach began.

"Understand this: Buying right can make you. Buying wrong can slow you down dramatically. If there is one thing you need to understand in real estate, it's how to negotiate well."

Sarah had always left negotiating to Brian; she was far too soft and always had sought to avoid anything that looked remotely confrontational. She knew she would have to address this if she was going to make a success of investing in the real estate market, but right now she was feeling so far out of her comfort zone that she was too petrified even to think about it.

Brian knew how she would be feeling and was concerned.

"Good negotiation will result in your achieving what you want regardless of the seller's circumstances," the Coach continued.

"Your job is to get your price or walk away! Remember, that's not the best price available; that's your price. There are always more deals out there waiting for you. Too many buyers pay too much for properties because they are not prepared to walk away from a deal. Auctions are a classic for this, and that's why agents love them!"

The Coach could sense that Sarah was beginning to feel uncomfortable.

"It's important to control your emotions and drive the negotiation process. You have the upper hand, after all. Remember, you're calling the shots; sit back and watch the seller react. You are very definitely in a position of strength, so use it wisely. Build into your offer everything you need to make it attractive to you."

Slowly Sarah asked, "Is this all about our winning and the seller losing, Coach?"

"I like to think of the negotiating process as the art of making the sellers happily give you what you want," he replied.

"So how do you do that?" she asked.

"Start off by fully understanding their motivation for selling. Listen very carefully to what the sellers or their agent say. Ask why they are selling. Is it to move out of town, because they are getting divorced, or upgrading to a larger house? Put yourself in their position and understand the pressures they would be under."

Sarah was beginning to understand.

"So it's about being empathetic, then."

"Very much so. And remember, a real estate agent will very often put words in the seller's mouth or represent the situation differently to package it in a much more politically correct way. But there is one thing agents are good at: *talking*. If you let them, they will go on for hours. Use the agents' weaknesses—their big mouths—and let them talk while you sweetly extract all the intelligence you need about the seller."

Sarah listened while Brian took notes.

"Having said that, I don't believe negotiating is a war. No one dies! Although I have caused a few heart attacks with some of my offers, no one has ever lost a limb."

Sarah was beginning to feel more and more relieved by the minute. She understood that this was a commercial transaction, and that both parties would be trying for as much as they could get, but at least it could be conducted civilly.

"I believe negotiating is nothing more than working through discussions—written or verbal—with the sellers until you understand what their real motivation for selling is," the Coach explained.

"Then you're home and dry. Understand this: As long as you satisfy their real reason for selling, they'll give in on everything else and often the price is the first casualty. It's human nature."

"Coach, can you give me an example?" Sarah wanted a little more reassurance.

"Sure. Think about a couple who advertised a house for $400,000, but when you negotiated you found out they had a tax payment they needed to make in 17 days. Could you make a much lower offer and, because of their time restrictions, they would sell to you for much less than the asking price?" The Coach turned it back to Sarah.

"Yes, now I see. Find their real reason for selling and a reason they would take less."

Brian was now a little puzzled, "So Coach, not everyone will have a reason to sell cheaply. Does that mean we just have to walk away?"

"Yes Brian, you'll walk away from more deals than you make."

Negotiation—
Because this strategy is about improving the capital
value, I really need to buy well. Negotiate hard,
negotiate long, and negotiate so that I buy at a price
where I will always make a profit.

"If you decide to buy at an auction, you need to be far more disciplined than normal, because it is a process that sells on the emotional level," the Coach explained.

"And as we all know, when you buy property as an investor, your buying decision is based on logic and not emotion. Putting this simply, the numbers have to stack up or it's a bad deal."

Brian was moving about uncomfortably in his chair now.

"You know, I've never felt comfortable about auctions, Coach," he said. "I have the feeling that I am not in control."

"That's exactly what the auctioneer wants, Brian. You see, most bidders find that very soon after the bidding starts, their egos get in the way and they end up bidding way more than they originally intended. See, most people are fairly competitive and can't stand the thought that someone else could beat them to the deal for the sake of a few hundred or thousand dollars. So they make one more bid—and then one more after that."

Brian thought for a moment and then added, "So auctions are not about winning, Coach?"

"No, it's like everything in investing, they are all about getting a great deal, Brian. And that means one in which your numbers stack up. Remember, you're buying wholesale, and it's the purchase price that will ultimately determine how much you make, not just the eventual selling price."

> **Auctions—**
> **Buying at auctions is a game. I need to manage my emotions, my bid, and my auction strategy. Bidding is not about winning; it's about a great deal. Sometimes when you win the auction, you lose on the deal.**

"But, Coach, if we use the traditional method of making an offer," Brian started, "how should we go about this? Do you have any advice for us?"

The Coach thought for a minute, then said, "Making offers needn't be an intimidating process for you. You see, you need to understand that when you decide to become real estate investors, one of the major strategies you will be using is the offer."

He paused to gather his thoughts.

"The idea here is not to assume anything. Don't make the mistake that so many do of thinking for the sellers or agents. Don't try to guess what they will be thinking, expecting, or wanting. See, you need to bear in mind that this is a game; they will be trying their best to only let you know what they want you to know. Even agents don't get told the full story by their vendors in most cases."

"So where does that leave us, Coach?" Sarah asked.

"In a very good position, Sarah. See, this means that what you have to do is to find out for yourself what they will really accept for their property. And the only way you can do this is by putting in offers. And often, lots of them."

"But what if they all get accepted, Coach? I mean, we certainly won't be able to buy above our capacity."

"Don't worry, Sarah. That won't happen because making offers is like shaking the tree to see what falls out. You will be testing the bottom limits of the price range to see what their real expectations are. You may only ever get one or two great deals in this price bracket, but these will be the ones where you will make handsome returns in the long run once you have renovated and redrawn from the increased equity they end up with. They are the ones you must be hunting for."

Brian understood.

"I get it, Coach. In order to ensure that the property has a decent amount of equity for us to redraw once we have renovated, we need to make sure our purchase price is as low as possible. And the only way to achieve this is to continually hunt suitable properties by making lower offers. This works because we just never know what the seller is willing to accept when presented with a written offer, and other things like timing or the fact that we offer a cash contract might sweeten the deal."

Brian felt proud of himself.

Making Offers—
My offers will depend on the market and how it's moving,
but I need to make offers regularly. Making an offer is like
shaking the tree just to see where the loose fruit is.

"When it comes to selecting the right property to buy," the Coach continued, "there are a number of things you need to bear in mind. How thorough you are here is going to make all the difference because you need to remember it's when you buy that you make your profit, not when you eventually sell. Do the right things now and you could be setting yourself up very nicely."

Brian smiled to himself; he certainly was on the right track here and that pleased him.

"It's more than just being at the right place at the right time, isn't it, Coach?" he responded. "I'm sure that helps, but how do you get to know where you need to be, and when?"

"Great question, Brian. This is what I recommend:

"First, track market trends. The first thing you need to understand when investing in real estate is what the market is doing. And remember, there's more than one real estate market. Different suburbs in different cities could be behaving vastly differently, and you need to understand this. Apart from the general economic trends, there are other equally important factors to bear in mind. For instance, if your chosen area has a leaning towards two single tenants living, but not sleeping together, you'd be looking for properties that have at least two double-sized bedrooms. Scan the Internet, and keep your eye on the local papers; after a while you'll start accumulating all sorts of useful information that will help crystallize your decision making."

Sarah was writing furiously.

"Second, study the available land supply in your chosen area. Real estate is all about supply and demand. Identify where the developers are working and ascertain the ramifications of their developments on supply and demand in your area. Be on the lookout for prime property, which will appreciate in time. Features that will ensure this are water frontage, river frontage, hills, views, and proximity to amenities and transport. This type of property is excellent for your 'long-term holds' and will traditionally provide great capital growth. If it's cashflow you're after, concentrate on the mid to low end of the market. Average properties in average neighborhoods usually work well. But don't exclude yourself from a diamond deal that is out there sitting in a capital growth hotspot and churning out cashflow at the same time. Those deals are much harder to find, but be open to them because you need to act *fast* when they come your way."

Brian was lapping this up.

"But how do we do this if the area we're targeting is new to us? You know, somewhere on the other side of the country, for instance," he asked.

"I always phone the president of the Real Estate Institute for that area or the top realtor and offer to pay for an hour or so of his or her time," the Coach replied.

"This way I get the inside track, and because this person is always a real estate agent, I've never been charged. I explain I'm seeking to buy some investment properties and need to know the current hot spots, market movements, trends, top capital growth and cashflow areas, and any other recommendations he or she might have. People like this are an encyclopedia of local property knowledge, so make sure you leverage their expertise and use every minute of your time with them wisely."

The Coach paused for Sarah's benefit.

"Third, you need to understand what I call the order of sale."

Brian looked up, puzzled.

"You need to understand how your chosen marketplace reacts when it starts moving. What types of properties sell first? What will follow? Normally, average houses go first because people moving into an area just want to get to know it better before buying a more expensive place. Once average homes start selling well, townhouses usually follow. Next will be development sites and 'renovator's delights.' These are the rules I've found to be true, but yours may be different, depending on the area you're operating in. Be guided by what you believe will happen in your area. If you want to buy a home to renovate, you need to jump into the market pretty early, otherwise you'll be looking for the proverbial needle in a haystack. This is why you need to understand the order of sale. Think back to what we discussed about buying the worst house on the best street."

Brian nodded.

"Buying, then renovating, and then redrawing the immediate capital gain is a great strategy for beginner investors in particular," the Coach went on, "and you can generally make good money if you don't pay too much and avoid risks like overcapitalizing or taking too long on the renovations."

Brian had stopped writing now. He had become immersed in the topic and didn't want to divide his attention. Besides, he knew that Sarah would be getting everything down accurately.

Evaluating—
This is the key skill of a great investor. I need
to evaluate everything from the suburb to the
rental per week and base my buy, renovate,
and redraw decisions on numbers, not emotions.

"The first thought when I look at renovating a property is who's going to buy or rent it. If I can ascertain this, then I'm in a good position to renovate the property so that it becomes attractive to these types of buyers or renters. Let's work through an example to illustrate this."

Sarah's ears pricked up. This approach appealed to her, as she instinctively knew it was the sensible thing to do. It was very similar in approach to the way she tackled most tasks that involved buying something that would eventually need to be sold or given away.

"Suppose I see a unit that I believe can be made attractive to a single woman. What are the features she would be looking for?"

"That's easy, Coach," Sarah responded. "Security, a lock-up garage with electric doors, a trendy appearance, and a private balcony or courtyard."

"OK, now if you know that, what renovations may need to be undertaken to make sure these key features are not only there in the first place, but up to her standards?"

The Coach paused and then went on: "Before I go ahead and start the renovations, I get a rental assessment on the unit from a local property manager to confirm what the rent would be if the unit were in its renovated state."

"Ah, I see the difference this would make, Coach," she said.

"In a few weeks we'll spend an entire session on renovations," the Coach said as he handed them his summary notes.

Renovating—
Basic rule of thumb is 10 percent of the price I paid
for the property, and more of a facelift than a renovation.
Remember, people rent the kitchen, the bathroom, and
the outside look. A good renovation will add between
20 and 40 percent value, and just as importantly,
a 20 to 40 percent increase in rental income.

"Next, I get an appraiser or a good realtor to give me a sale price assessment of the unit based on my anticipated improvements. This will confirm the likely redraw options I will have when the job is done," the Coach continued.

"The aim of the game is to be able to add value to my purchase by renovating enough to satisfy what my target market wants; this will put the property in a higher rental bracket than it was before renovations began."

Sarah was excited.

"So this will immediately mean more cashflow, Coach."

"Yes, as well as a higher redraw facility because its value will be higher, resulting in my having more equity in the property. The aim now is to redraw as much as you can of this equity so that you get most of your cash outlay back. You may then end up with a property that owes you little if anything."

"Coach, I'm not sure I understand what you mean by redraw," Brian admitted with a puzzled look on his face.

"OK, first, the term redraw means to draw out your cash or capital from the property after your renovation. So, for example, let's say you bought a house at $200,000. According to your rules, that means the house should be worth at least $220,000 right?"

Brian nodded.

"So, when you go in and renovate, how much can you invest as a maximum according to my rules on the renovation, Brian?" The Coach was on a roll.

"Ten percent of the purchase price, or $20,000, Coach," he said with confidence.

"Great, so after the renovation you'll raise the rent and have a higher income, with all the changes, the higher rent, and so on, you'll have increased the value, right?"

Now both Brian and Sarah were nodding with the Coach.

"So initially the house was bought for $200,000, at 80 percent LVR, you put in how much cash Sarah?" The Coach was giving Sarah a shot at answering.

"$40,000 to buy it and $20,000 to renovate, so a total of $60,000, Coach."

"Great thinking team, so let's assume you had done your numbers right, got the renovation done on budget and on time and after everything, your new valuation was up from $220,000 when you bought it to $290,000. That's just under a 32 percent increase in value overall and you can now go back to your bankers. What would they do, do you think?" the Coach was again making them think.

Brian started, "Well Coach, if it's new value was $290,000, then we could loan 80 percent of that as long as we could service it, and the new rent would help with that, so I guess we could get out . . ."

"$232,000," Sarah blurted as she had already done the math, "so we could pay back our previous loan of $160,000 and get our $60,000 redrawn with $12,000 left over to cover costs, use on the next deal, or simply leave in as equity."

"Wow," said Brian, "I like the look of those sorts of deals."

"Great, Brian, but remember, they don't just grow on trees. You have to look hard, negotiate well, do your numbers, and renovate well, but they do exist and many people have started their entire property portfolio just this way. Remember, you now have your $60,000 back to go and do another deal just like it."

"So, Coach, is there a particular type of loan we can get to do this that will make is easy?" Sarah smiled with excitement as she asked.

"Some banks have renovator loans where you won't have to pay fees when you redraw at the end, but most of all, negotiate with your bankers on the fees for the redraw. The last thing you want is to lose your profits in fees." The Coach again handed Brian and Sarah his note on the subject.

Refinance—
**The key is to add enough value to get your *cash*
back from each deal. Rather than sell, refinance
and hold long term with none—or very little—
of your own cash still left in the deal.**

"The final things we need to discuss this session are your long-term finance loan structures as opposed to the redraw style loans," the Coach said.

"The main thing to bear in mind all along is to take care of your cashflow as well as your borrowing capacity. See, it's all very well to be asset rich, as most property investors are, but the sad thing is that this usually also means they are cash poor."

Sarah could identify with this; she had seen it happen to one of her friends over the years. It was probably one of the major reasons that stopped her from taking an interest in these matters a long time ago.

"It is important to structure your plan in such a way that you hang on to both your cashflow or your borrowing capacity because by doing so, you will always remain in a position to add to your portfolio whenever the opportunity arises," the Coach continued.

"But how can we do this if we don't have huge cash reserves, Coach?" Sarah asked.

"By carefully planning, Sarah," the Coach replied.

Brian nodded as he wrote.

"So let's start from the beginning. You have equity in your own home, so you can use that for your first investment property, or you can take a little longer and save a deposit. Either way, this is where your investing starts," the Coach was trying to move slowly through a rather complex subject and make it as simple as he could.

"But, Coach, what about those late-night infomercials that promise 'no-money-down deals' and so on?" Sarah wanted to know more.

"Yes, team, they are definitely possible, and as you get more experienced in investing you will start to do them too, but I wouldn't recommend that novice investors buy properties with 100 percent financing. It makes you seriously negative in cashflow and puts you in a situation where after two or three deals you have no ability to borrow any more."

"Oh, I didn't realize they had to be 100 percent financed," Brian noted.

"Brian, no money down deals usually require part bank financing, about 80 percent, and the other 20 percent comes from other sources. If you have equity in your own home, you can do a no-money-down deal in essence," he explained. But the Coach wanted to get back to the topic rather than get novice investors building their dreams on negative cashflow that they couldn't sustain.

"So, back to the topic." The Coach took a deep breath before continuing, "There's another thing you could do. Remember what we discussed about the Property Wealth Wheels? Well, structure your affairs, loans, and companies or trusts around them. Remember to get good accounting and legal advice in each state or country you invest in here as tax and investing laws for different entities are different everywhere."

Brian was writing as fast as he could.

"I very rarely include more than one Property Wealth Wheel in one entity, and I structure my loans accordingly," the Coach continued. "The reason for this is that if there is something that goes wrong, I risk losing no more than I need to, as my Wealth Wheels aren't connected."

Brian whistled in appreciation while he wrote. "I had better get our advisors to help us out with this in detail then, Coach."

"Every loan I have for my positive cashflow properties is *interest only.* I know banks will pressure you to make deposits against the principal and take principal and interest loans as well, because it's this money they use to lend to others. But I resist and will take my business elsewhere if necessary. I usually aim to refinance and redraw from my properties after five or so years anyway."

Brian nodded.

"Now, onto our capital growth or negatively geared deals. With these I use what's referred to as a revolving line of credit, or a 100 percent offset mortgage where every dollar in the account for a day reduces the principle and therefore the interest for that day," the Coach started to notice his students were getting a little overloaded.

"So team, what do you think the advantage of this might be?" he asked.

They immediately sprung to life, wanting to come up with a solid answer. It was Sarah who spoke first.

"Coach, it's like in my business: if I have a smaller overdraft I pay less interest. Over a long period of time, such as 20 years or so of a house loan, it will add up to a massive difference in total interest."

"So you were listening," the Coach began. "And on top of all that, if you structure your Wealth Wheel right, you will have all the rents going into the line of credit loan and just that few extra days of reduced balance will make a huge difference long term.

"But let's now think about another very good reason for keeping your own cash investment in property as low as possible. It's called leverage, which is all about doing more with less. If you have $10,000 in cash, you can buy property in a price range between $50,000 and $100,000. Understand that $50,000 going up by 10 percent gives you a $5000 return. So if you only have $10,000 invested, that's a 50 percent return on cash invested."

Brian scribbled furiously, trying to work this out for himself.

"Real estate is generally only a good investment if it's leveraged. If it isn't, it's pretty ordinary. You see, a business or shares will generally provide you with much higher rates of returns than real estate will if you invest 100 percent cash, but how much can you borrow against a business? You'd be doing very well indeed if you could borrow 60 percent of your stock value."

"I see what you mean, Coach," he said.

"Spend some time thinking about how you can structure your financing to your advantage. It may mean you need to refinance existing properties. Often this can make the difference between an ordinary deal and a super one. And don't forget personal loans or credit cards; most banks have facilities for these, so consider them as you start your investing and need to renovate."

Sarah nodded.

"There seem to be far more options available to us that I really hadn't even thought of, Coach," she commented.

"By looking after your cash reserves, you look after your borrowing capacity. If you establish a term deposit through which you finance your property purchases, you can use it over and over again without any trouble at all. And you keep control of your money."

Brian and Sarah were upbeat as they drove home. They were beginning to think like property investors already.

Long-Term Finance Loan Structures—
Positive cashflow deals should use interest-only
loans over as long a time frame as I can get, and capital
growth deals should use an offset or revolving credit
mortgage facility so I can manage my cashflow,
my fees, and my borrowing capacity.

$$\boxed{\textbf{Part 6}}$$

∎ Profit at Purchase

Brian knew that the profit they make on any investment property would be determined by the purchase price. The Coach had made mention of this a few times now. Sarah had remarked that this made the negotiation process all the more important.

It also made her a little more nervous.

Brian kept reassuring her that it wasn't a case of being nasty or anything like that; it was merely a business transaction and that was the way they had to view it. This also highlighted the importance of doing their homework properly. It also highlighted the importance of having their own clearly defined set of rules.

They were still discussing this when they pulled up outside the Coach's office, parked, and made the way to his front door.

"Hello, folks, come on in," the Coach said as he opened the door. "And how are you?"

"We're just fine, Coach," Brian replied as he followed Sarah in.

"Today we are going to go through some of the variables that will help ensure your real estate purchases are as profitable to you as possible right at the time of purchase. After all, getting a return is the sole reason we invest in real estate, isn't it?"

"When you come to think of it, I guess that's it, Coach," Sarah responded. It made it sound so mercenary, yet logical at the same time.

They took their seats in the now-familiar office and sat back, waiting to hear what pearls of wisdom the Coach had for them. Brian was fairly sure a few more common misconceptions were about to go out the window.

He was right.

"The game begins right at the beginning, when you find a suitable property that meets the requirements of your plan and the conditions of your rules. The first thing you do at this stage is fill in an offer to purchase. Now bear in mind that what happens next is like a game. The seller will have a price in mind and so will you. The only difference is the seller's will be based on emotion while yours will be based on an investor's logic."

The Coach paused, then continued.

"This is potentially disastrous because as you know, these prices can be worlds apart. The seller will have built in some room to maneuver on the advertised or listed price, and your task is to find out what the limit is. The last thing you want to happen is for the seller—or the agent for that matter—to get you to start dealing on an emotional level as well, because this would mean that you would no longer be objective in your decision making."

"So we must start off offering low," Sarah added. "We need to shake the tree to see what falls out."

"You learn fast, Sarah. But there's something else to bear in mind here; you must negotiate hard. Don't buckle. Stick to your game plan and stick to the numbers. If the numbers don't stack up, resist the temptation to try and rework them so they do fit. I would rather walk away from the deal; there are thousands more on the market."

Negotiation—
Often people will be willing to sell at a perceived or real discount if I can offer them some other benefit like a short time frame. I need to negotiate hard, bearing in mind that the deal must satisfy my numbers or it is not a viable proposition, no matter how nice the property seems.

"It's often a case of thinking outside the box to get a fantastic deal," the Coach continued.

"This is why I prefer to negotiate direct with the seller rather than thirdhand through the agent if at all possible. See, most agents aren't trained for this; they just do it the same old way time and time again."

Sarah was intrigued.

"What kind of things do you have in mind here, Coach?" she asked. Apart from being genuinely interested, she was fascinated by the Coach's creativeness.

"First it might be a simple twist in the way the house is built or kept, like completely removing gardens so it has better street appeal. Or changing a window into a doorway so people can reach a new deck or their backyard even easier. These are things to look for as a buyer.

Brian had watched dozens of the renovation TV shows so he knew a lot of what the Coach was referring to.

"Next, it could be a twist on the way you finance the deal. You might even pay a portion to the owner over time; that's commonly called seller financing. You could even play dumb and ask the seller to help you put the deal together. Sellers will generally not say no because their egos will get in the way.

"I've even put deals together where I have taken possession and renovated before I took ownership and settled the deal. Now I know this is a little risky for most new investors, but I just want you to know that sometimes you have to start to really look for a twist to see how you can make a deal come together and still meet your rules."

Sarah was really starting to think of how her creative deal-making would help her out to no end here.

"Another few things I've done is make an offer to buy a house that included a TV and a car, just so the seller had something to focus on other than the price. Or, I've created a twist by buying a property and then furnishing it with furniture from garage sales to increase the rental and make a negatively geared deal into a positive cashflow one."

"Coach, that's brilliant, and I'll bet you didn't pay much for the furniture either." Brian was thinking of how his bartering skills would come in handy.

"No, just a couple of thousand furnished a two-bedroom property." The Coach finished up with his usual notes.

> ### See a Twist—
> **Always look for an opportunity others miss. Putting together a deal in a different way very often is the difference between achieving a great deal and achieving nothing at all. Lateral thinking may be all it takes.**

"Another way to ensure you come across the great deals is to make sure you are always in the market," the Coach explained.

"What do you mean by that, Coach?" Sarah asked, not sure that she understood the statement correctly.

"Let me explain it this way, Sarah. Deals don't just appear; they won't miraculously come your way just because you are an investor."

Sarah nodded. This much she knew.

"You need to actively be working the market. By this I mean you should make sure you are talking to real estate agents all the time. See, they move on if you stop calling them. It is seldom that one will keep you on file in case something you are after comes along. Now I know they will tell you they will, but my experience is they seldom will. So make it your business to keep in touch. Call them regularly. This way you will remain foremost in their minds.

"One last point here: Build a list of Realtors you speak with often, and keep them up-to-date with what you're doing. Remember they're on your team." Another note came quickly from the Coach.

> ### Timing—
> **I've got to always be in the market so that at some stage I will be in the right place at the right time. Often being first to a deal is the difference between good and great.**

"Another thing you need to remember as far as the eventual profit you'll make from your real estate purchases is this: It's all about the value of the land you are buying. Sure, the building has value, but remember we discussed that buildings depreciate over time whereas land goes up in value."

Sarah remembered well, and nodded.

"If you can get a great deal on the price of the building, with the land value being reasonable, then you stand a good chance of profiting well. So know your land values. Do your homework well here; it will pay off."

Sarah still wanted more. "So, we work out our purchase price based on the land value alone?"

"Not entirely. I simply look for deals where I can buy both the land and the building for the value of the land alone," the Coach said as he passed yet another note. The session was flying by today.

**Land Value—
It's all about the value of the ground under the
building I buy. If I know what land sells for, then I can
see how much I'm paying for the building.**

"Making a profit when you buy can sometimes happen just because you know what it is you're looking for. The more you know about your area, the better," the Coach explained. "This is vitally important because you really are buying something from somebody who has an emotional attachment to what she is selling."

"So how do we get around that, Coach?" Sarah asked.

"The only way is to increase your knowledge base. And that means getting out there and seeing as much in your chosen market as you can. Talk to the various stakeholders like estate agents, landlords, attorneys, bankers, brokers, and appraisers. Do this for just a few weekends and you'll find you'll soon develop a pretty good picture of what the market is doing.

"Next come the books, magazines, and Web sites you can consult to get as much information as you can. Remember that risk is all about lack of knowledge." And yet another note came from the Coach as he finished.

> **Knowledge—**
> The more I know, the less I risk. If I know market values
> then I can make a deal where others don't see a deal at all.
> The more I know about the market, the better my
> decisions will be.

"In times when the market is slow, this is when you can really make some good deals. And that means profit."

Brian looked up in surprise.

"Why would we make high profits when the market is down, Coach?" he asked.

"Remember what I said about profit being determined by your buying price and not your selling price, Brian?"

Brian nodded; he remembered that very well because it came as something of a surprise.

"Let me put it this way: What is a slow market?"

"It's one where there are more sellers than buyers, Coach."

"Exactly. And that means you hold the trump card. It's a time when you really do get to call the shots. And remember, sellers still need to sell for whatever reason. Life for them must go on. They don't stop just because the market is slow. See, this could be providing them with other opportunities which they have decided they need to take."

Brian nodded.

"So this is when you come in with really low offers. It's all about shaking the tree, only this time you stick to staying low. Get a really low offer accepted and when the market turns, as it invariably does, you get to profit generously."

> ## No One's Buying—
> It's time to lowball and negotiate harder than ever, stick
> with my first offer, and don't get sucked into paying too
> much. Remember, I have the upper hand in times like this.

"So what do we need to do during boom times to ensure we still have a chance of making a decent profit, Coach?" Brian asked. "I mean, during times like these when everyone is buying whatever comes on the market, are there still bargains to be had?"

"There certainly are, Brian," the Coach replied. "You may have to work a little harder to find them and you may also have to negotiate more, but they are there."

Sarah looked pensive.

"Does this mean we have to have strong nerves?"

"No, not at all. You need to take a broader view of things, Sarah. You may need to alter your game plan a little to allow for much longer settlement periods, for instance."

"How is that going to make any difference, Coach?" she asked.

"One of the distinguishing factors of a boom market is the fact that prices rise very quickly due to supply and demand considerations. Now you may have to pay well above what you normally would for a property because the market is booming, but remember what we said some time ago—your profit is based on your purchase price and not your selling price. This means the price at purchase relative to the going rate at the time. So if you have your purchase price agreed by the seller at the time you make your offer, but only take ownership sometime later down the track—let's say three months—then it is only at this time, when the deal settles, that your bank hands over the agreed amount of money. And what has happened to the going rate of properties on the market in the meantime?"

"They are rising pretty quickly, Coach, because of supply and demand factors," Brian replied.

"That's right. So now how would your agreed purchase price stack up against a new, higher market price? Probably quite well, I would think. Your purchase price would now be looking a whole lot more reasonable, wouldn't it?"

Everyone's Buying—
Bargains are still to be had when there's a
buying frenzy going on. I just have to work a little
harder. Usually the market is booming so I really
want a long settlement period.

"So what do we do when the market is neither slow nor booming, Coach?" Sarah asked. She could understand the logic of these two markets, but wasn't sure where that would leave them in those in-between times.

"Great question, Sarah. What do you think you should do?"

She thought for a moment and then looked at Brian as if looking for his support. She didn't find it. He avoided her glance, as he too wasn't quite sure what to do.

After an awkward moment, she suddenly said, "I wouldn't feel comfortable doing anything, Coach, so I would sit back and wait."

The Coach smiled, pleased with her frankness.

"And you'd be doing the right thing, Sarah. Remember, the trend is your friend. There are times when it is best to sit on the sidelines and wait for the market to make up its mind which way it is going. See, how can you make informed decisions when all the market variables are constantly changing? This would be the time to consolidate what you have and prepare for action in the next phase of the market, whatever that would be.

"One other thing I do in this time is renovate or refurbish some of my older properties just to keep busy." And another note came from the Coach.

"By the way, how do we know when the market is turning?" the Coach questioned.

Brian was quick to answer. "We should already see it happening as we are watching the market very closely, Coach."

"And the newspapers, Coach," Sarah added, "There may be articles, like 'When will this growth spurt end?' to signal the end of the boom times a little early."

"Great thinking, team."

A Jittery Market—
Special consideration needs to be given when
the market doesn't quite know what it is doing.
Remember, sometimes the best way to play the game
is to watch from the sidelines.

"There is another factor that will affect the amount of profit you derive from your investment properties," the Coach said, making sure his students weren't overloaded with information as the session proceeded into its final stage in record time.

"And it relates to the price you buy at, too."

Sarah was thoroughly enjoying the session. She had only just realized that she hadn't been taking down notes as diligently as she usually did because she had immersed herself in the subject matter so much this time.

"Think what shop owners do when they buy their stock. How do they buy?"

"They buy wholesale, Coach," she replied.

"That's exactly right, Sarah. So do you think you could make extra profit from buying real estate wholesale as opposed to retail?"

She thought for a moment and then replied, "I know you've shown us this before, but I'm not sure that Brian and I can buy property that way, Coach."

She glanced over to Brian, and he nodded in agreement.

"Think of the stock market. Who makes the *real* money there?"

Brian sat up and replied quickly; this was an area he knew something about.

"Wholesale investors because they usually have access to stock before it is available to ordinary investors. They buy at discounted rates and they usually don't even have to pay high stockbroking fees, especially if they are offered shares directly by the listed institution."

"That's right, Brian. And when they get to sell, the price they get is usually terrific because they bought low. They make more profit than ordinary investors who may have bought the same stock, even at the same time, but they paid retail."

Brian nodded. He could tell that Sarah was following where this was going.

"So if we could buy properties wholesale, they would be even more profitable for us."

"That's right. So how do you buy wholesale?"

"That was my original question, Coach," Sarah responded.

"Let's look at it this way: Ordinary property buyers are your retail buyers, aren't they? They buy the normal way through agents. They pay the market price and compete against other buyers on the open market. Nothing surprising here. And this isn't the way investors should buy if they can help it. See, this market is driven by emotion, and investors should be buying on logic. So they need to not buy retail for this reason too."

"So where do we find the wholesale market, Coach?" Brian asked, still a little baffled.

"One way is to deal directly with the seller and not through the agent, who will be working you against other buyers, usually retail buyers who are willing to be driven by emotional considerations. If you have to go through an agent, then you could get in early before the market kicks in. To do this you need to get close to the agent and have her as part of your team.

"Now I'm not suggesting anything sinister here; only you need to make contact with good ones and let them know that you are an investor who is looking for lots of property. You could tell them you have an insatiable appetite for investment properties and as such, you want to be the first to know as soon as a new property is listed so you can make a quick move if it is suitable. This way you get to avoid competing with the retail buyers and the sellers get a quick sale, which could be what they are after.

"Another very popular way to do this is to team up with other investors and buy as a group from a developer, or even eventually develop deals yourself, keeping some as long-term rentals.

"Remember, developers have two times they really want to sell, the first few and the last few, so help them out." The Coach smiled as he thought of several deals where developers had courted him so he would invest in their deals.

They had covered a lot of ground during the session and were beginning to feel the effects of concentrating for long periods of time. As a result, Sarah looked relieved when the Coach said that was all he had wanted to discuss and would see them again next week.

Buying Wholesale versus Retail—
I *never* want to pay retail. I can buy wholesale
the same way I would for anything else, by buying
directly from the supplier and buying in bulk. And
remember, if I don't have to compete with the "retail"
market, emotions won't drive up the price.

Part 7

▌Buy on the Numbers

Brian was beginning to feel as if he really understood what being a real estate investor was all about. The last few sessions had been particularly useful in dispelling a few myths he had been harboring for years. And the more he learned, the more he realized that he could do this, and do it well.

He knew that Sarah was feeling the same way because they discussed it often enough. In fact, they found they had a new topic to discuss whenever they had the chance, now that they had a Coach.

Sarah in particular felt she had learned a lot. She was also becoming a lot more confident.

The days leading up to their next coaching session were spent discussing some of the key things they had learned. One of those was that real investors bought based on the numbers. They didn't allow themselves to get caught up in all the emotional stuff.

So it was with more than a little anticipation and enthusiasm that they made their way to the Coach's office for their next session. It was to be all about buying on the numbers, and they were keen to hear what else the Coach had to tell them.

"The one thing I want you to understand as real estate investors," the Coach said as he started off the session, "is that it all comes down to the numbers; it's not about windows, floors, or bathrooms, but numbers. And not just one number but all of them when viewed over the long term."

Brian nodded and began to write.

It's All about the Numbers—
Property investment is all about the numbers,
but it's more than any one single number alone. I must
truly understand what my returns will be over time.

"Let's assume you have $150,000 that you want to invest. Suppose you were to deposit this in a bank account. Let's also suppose it was your lucky day and you locked the money up at an interest rate of 7 percent. Write this down:

INVESTMENT	= $150,000
INTEREST EARNED	= 7%
INCOME	= $10,500

"Now let's assume you are on an income tax rate of 30 percent; this is similar to the top tax rate for many countries. Again, write this down:

TAX PAYABLE	= $3,150
NET INCOME	= $7,350
NET RETURN	= 4.9%

Or, put another way . . . 7% less 30% tax = 4.9%

"This isn't the end of the story. Let's now assume *inflation* to be running at 3 percent. Our net return after inflation is therefore only 1.9 percent. That's a 1.9 percent return after tax and inflation."

"At this rate it would take more than 40 years to double your money. I'd rather double it every 10 years. And through following the rules and working hard at investing in real estate, you can."

Brian was impressed. He had always known that cash in the bank was a poor investment, but he hadn't known just how poor it really is from an investment point of view.

"So let's now look at how you'd fare if you took that same $150,000 and bought a property instead of putting it in the bank," the Coach went on.

"Again, for the sake of comparison, we will make a few basic assumptions. Let's assume the $150,000 property represents fair or market value. Let's also assume this property returns a very conservative rental income of $150 a week. How do the figures now look? Write these down:

INVESTMENT = **$150,000**

INCOME (Rent of $150 per week) = **$7,500**

"Now let's again assume you are on an income tax rate of 30 percent.

TAX RATE (assume no deductions) = **$2,250**

NET INCOME = **$5,250**

"Now we need to make another very conservative assumption, this time on the rate of capital growth.

CAPITAL GROWTH (7%) = **$10,500**

TOTAL NET INCOME = **$15,750**

"If we were to now look at our after-tax return on equity, we get a very respectable 10.5 percent."

"Is this an accurate figure, Coach?" Brian asked.

"A stock broker will show you this as a 5 percent yield, which he would calculate by dividing the $7500 rental return by the $150,000 property price," he explained.

"This is not correct, as it assumes there is no capital growth. I'm never interested in the yield of a property because I never pay cash for it in the first place. It's the stupidest thing to do. If you own your own home outright, please reconsider your thinking, as it amounts to not using your assets to build your wealth. The major advantage real estate has over other investment strategies is the ability to leverage a small amount of capital into a large investment."

Brian leaned back in his chair, ran his fingers through his hair, and whistled quietly to himself. He could see where the Coach was going.

Not Yields—
Brokers will try to compare stocks and property yields.
Yield is nothing more than the rental income compared
with the property value and is *not* a good indicator for
property investment.

"Again, let's see how the figures would pan out if you took the same $150,000 and bought a house, at fair value, but this time leveraged with 85 percent financing. Let's assume you secured the loan at a high interest rate of 9 percent, and that, once again, you were to receive 7 percent yield or only able to get $150 a week in rent from a tenant. Again, write this down:

DEPOSIT	= $22,500
BORROW	= $127,500
INTEREST PAID (9%)	= $11,475
INCOME (Rent $150 per week)	= $7,500
PRETAX Negative Cashflow	= −$3,975
TAX REBATE (assume no other deductions)	= $1,192.50
CASH CONTRIBUTION NEEDED	= $2,782.50
CAPITAL GROWTH (7%)	= $10,500
NET TOTAL RETURN	= $7,717.50

"To calculate your after-tax return on equity, you work this out on your capital invested, which in this case is your deposit.

AFTER-TAX RETURN ON EQUITY = 34.3%

"Now let's consider what would happen if you were to go the whole hog and borrow the full amount to buy this $150,000 house."

DEPOSIT	= $0
BORROW	= $150,000
INTEREST PAID (9%)	= $13,500
INCOME (Rent $150 per week)	= $7,500
PRETAX Negative Cashflow	= –$6,000
Tax Rebate (30%) (assume no other deductions)	= $1,800
CASH CONTRIBUTION NEEDED	= $4,200
CAPITAL GROWTH (7%)	= $10,500
NET TOTAL RETURN	= $6,300

"In this case, to calculate your after-tax return on equity, you'd compare your net total return with the total amount of cash you contributed ($6300 divided by $4200).

AFTER-TAX RETURN ON EQUITY = 150%

"Of course I am using depreciation and tax rates solely to illustrate this example. The investment principles taught in this example are universally applicable in every country in the world."

Brian nodded. He understood the power of examples only too well.

Not Growth Rates—
Capital growth rates from around the world are quoted
between 6 percent and 11 percent, but again, this is only
part of the property investment equation.

"The challenge here is that you're getting this fabulous rate of return on the small amount of money you contributed during the year. But as part of a balanced portfolio, this will work exceptionally well. I don't like negative gearing generally, but if I must, I set up a property to give me this sort of return as part of my portfolio. I'll be quite happy to do it, as long as it's not me that's contributing to the loss on the property."

Sarah looked up from her notes, sucked on the end of her pen for a moment while she gathered her thoughts, and then said: "Coach, I thought negatively geared investments were really popular."

"You need to be clear on why you want to negatively gear a property in the first place," the Coach replied. "Many people choose this option simply for the tax advantages and not the profit it will produce. I wouldn't buy property to make a loss to reduce my tax; the profit should be on the property.

"You see, at the end of the financial year, some accountants advise people to reduce their tax bill by buying a negatively geared property. But let me ask you, would you buy a business that was running at a loss, purely because it would give you a tax break on the other income you already made?" The Coach didn't even wait for a reply.

It was time for a short break. The Coach passed over their notes and allowed them to stretch their legs and settle their minds. He was careful not to overload them with too much information at once this time.

Not Tax Benefits—
One of the least important reasons to invest in property is
tax deductions. While I love getting depreciation, interest,
and other costs as deductibles from my other income, I buy
property to make money, *not* to lose it so I get a deduction.

"One of the important things about being a real estate investor is that you need to consider your investment numbers in their entirety," the Coach began.

Sarah looked up and nodded. She had long since realized that there was more to it than rental income. And she had also learned that in this game there could be some surprises.

"Now, team, we've seen what I'm about to show you here before, but as it's the most important number you can possibly know in your investment decision, I want to make sure you know how to calculate it." The Coach was extremely forthright about this point.

Brian sat up, ready to take it all in. He even had his pen ready this time.

"I want to teach you how to work out your investments' Internal Rate of Return, or IRR for short.

"It will probably feel a little complex at first, but stay with me and you'll soon see that it's relatively easy. First comes your cashflow from rental income, then there's the growth in the total value, the tax benefits, the costs, the inflation, and the total cash you invested."

Sarah had pulled out the Coach's last example from his notes about the $150,000 house, so she had something to refer to.

"So, Coach, back in this example the IRR was 34.3 percent and then with 100 percent financing it was 150 percent," she showed Brian her notes as she spoke.

"Correct, and what parts of the complete IRR formula did we leave out?" Coach asked.

"Well, we didn't look at inflation of the rental income or the costs, and we didn't add in any deductions for depreciation or other tax benefits," Sarah added.

Brian whistled in surprise. There was more to being an investor than he had imagined.

"I see what you mean, Coach," he said. "The overall result in this case is pretty stunning. And as you say, that's the number it is all about. Is there an easy way to work this out, Coach?"

"Yes. I use some simple property investor software that calculates IRR for me over 10 years. You can usually find a local program that will use your state or country taxes provided by your local Property Investors Association."

The Coach spent the next 20 minutes showing Brian and Sarah his software and recommended they research for themselves to see what else was available that might be newer and better than the Coach's program.

He then passed them his next note.

Internal Rate of Return = Cashflow, Plus Growth, Plus Benefits to Cash Invested—
It's the total investment package that is appealing, not just one aspect of it. My Internal Rate of Return measures the return for the *cash* I put in to the total return with rent, capital growth, costs, and taxation benefits all combined. If I truly want to evaluate a property investment, I have to follow this formula.

"Before we finish up for the day, I want to go back and reinforce two of the most important rules of buying an investment property," the Coach said, making sure to pause long enough for the gravity of what he was about to say to sink in.

"It's all about the numbers. Nothing else counts."

"That's why we must take care never to slip to the emotional level," Sarah added without thinking.

"That's right, Sarah, the agent will naturally want to impress you with the features of the property, but they are just emotive things," the Coach replied. "You need to judge the property solely on the deal. If the numbers stack up, then go for it; if they don't, move on and look for something else."

> **Ignore Aesthetics—**
> **The property's looks and aesthetics have to do**
> **with emotion; investing in real estate is a logical**
> **numbers decision, not an emotive one.**

"And the second point is that if you do allow yourself to slip to the emotional level when looking at a property, then you will run the risk of judging it against the same criteria you would when looking for a new home for yourself to live in."

The Coach paused so that Sarah could complete her notes.

"You know, concerns such as are the bedrooms large enough? What about the size of the built-in cupboards? I really can't stand the bathroom; the tiles are so 1970s."

Sarah was laughing now; she knew exactly what he meant, as this typified the way she always bought.

"Remember, you don't have to live there. Just because you wouldn't live in the place doesn't mean someone else won't love it. It's like the cars we drive. Some people would never be seen dead in a station wagon, yet others wouldn't have anything else."

They had reached the end of another busy and informative session. Brian felt drained and exhilarated at the same time. Sarah felt relieved because by understanding the 'buy on the numbers' principle, she would be in a better position to negotiate effectively without compromising her moral beliefs, which she had originally thought would be limiting in this game.

> **You Don't Have to Live There—**
> **Never make the mistake of disregarding a property just**
> **because you wouldn't live there. You don't have to,**
> **and others may love it. In fact, often the best investments**
> **wouldn't suit your lifestyle.**

Part 8

■ Cosmetic Only, No Structural

Brian was looking forward to their next session; it was going to be all about renovating, and as an avid do-it-yourselfer, he couldn't wait to hear what the Coach had to say on the topic.

It wasn't that he intended to do all the renovations himself, but he knew he could save himself a lot of money and really kick-start his investing future by doing all of the simple tasks and leaving the complex ones to the professionals.

Sarah too was interested in this aspect of real estate. She liked the idea of increasing the value of a property by planning and carrying out some renovation work to improve its appeal. Especially as she knew she could make each house look great, even on their small budget.

She quietly hoped this would be the catalyst to get things moving with their own home. She had been dreaming of modernizing their bathroom for so long she had all but given up. There always seemed to be other, more pressing things that got in the way.

"Today we are going to be thinking about what it is you should and shouldn't do when renovating investment properties," the Coach began. He leaned back in his chair and waited for Sarah to flip open her notebook and begin writing.

"It's important to understand that the renovation process actually starts long before the tradesmen arrive on site."

He looked at Brian as he spoke as if he were addressing his comments directly to him. Brian picked up on this and asked, "When does it start then, Coach?"

"It starts when you are still inspecting the property prior to starting the negotiation process."

Sarah looked up in surprise.

"What you are in fact doing at this stage is selecting properties that only require cosmetic work," the Coach replied before she had a chance to ask why.

"One of the things you'll be looking for are properties that are basically sound structurally. You really want to avoid places that require any structural work done at all because you never really know where this will end. One thing always leads to another when the builder gets going. It's much like rust in a car; you may only see some evidence of rust around the wheel arches and sills, but when you cut away the rotten metal, it invariably reveals other rusted sections that weren't there before."

Brian nodded. He knew exactly what the Coach was talking about.

"Foundation work with houses is very unpredictable and so is termite damage in timber. From a cost estimate point of view, it's very difficult to budget for as well. My experience is that costs usually blow out, so it's better to stay clear of properties that look as though they will need any sort of structural work done at all."

**Structural Means Problems—
One structural defect usually leads to another and another, and so on. Structural repair takes more time and more money than you ever expect. Avoid properties that require structural repairs at all costs.**

"Speaking of budgets, how much should be put aside for renovations, Coach?" Sarah asked. She looked up only briefly enough to show she was participating in the discussion, then readied herself to take notes once more.

"Remember, I usually recommend about 10 percent of the purchase price, Sarah. So work on $20,000 if you bought for $200,000."

"Why so low, though?" she asked.

"Don't think of it as being low. Think of it as being a rough guide to stop you from falling into the trap of overcapitalizing on the property. This is one of the single biggest pitfalls investors fall into. It results in their losing money. And if you are in this to make money, losing money is the last thing you want to do."

"So, Coach, does that mean that sometimes we'll need to do some of the work ourselves?" Brian was starting to get excited at the thought of actually working with his hands.

"Yes, some of my students even team up with other couples who are looking to grow their wealth and help each other out on weekends. Just remember that some jobs are faster and cheaper with a professional, though."

**Ten Percent for Cosmetic—
A good rule-of-thumb guide to how much to spend on cosmetic work is 10 percent of the purchase price. Don't get carried away or you will overcapitalize and lose money.**

"What are the most important rooms in the home, Sarah?" the Coach asked, knowing full well what she would say.

"I'd say the kitchen and the bathrooms, Coach." He smiled as he nodded. Women always chose those rooms, and they were right.

"And they are particularly important in a rental property, Sarah. The kitchen is the most important of the two, so I'll talk about it first. Get this room right and your property becomes so much more rentable. And that means you can get a higher rent for it."

"So how far do we go when tackling the kitchen, Coach?" Brian asked.

"Plan on doing a good job here. Most often you will find it cheaper to completely remove the entire thing and start again, especially if you work with companies that cut all the cabinetry and counters to size for you, so all you have to do is put it all together."

Brian had helped a friend with one of these so knew exactly what the Coach was referring to.

"Next is to get more light into the room, and generally a bigger window or removing a wall is all it takes. Then it's all about updating the appliances and the fixtures.

"If you do decide to only do a part of the kitchen, then retile or repaint the walls and retile or replace the floor covering. Pay attention to the cupboards and benchtops, and add more power sockets and storage spaces wherever possible. You might even need to make the space for a fridge even bigger. Oh, and remember the lighting and fire alarm."

Sarah made notes as Brian listened.

"Do the job so it lasts for around 10 years. That way you won't have to do it again. But be careful you stick within your budget, as this is one room where you can easily overspend if you aren't careful."

"Coach, would most of our budget go to this room, then?" Sarah was just checking her thinking.

"Probably not most of it, but it along with the bathroom will be the biggest percentage spenders of all."

Kitchens—
Kitchens are the most important room in a rental
property. A complete overhaul that will last 10 to 12 years
is a must. Remember to stay in budget, though.

"So now to the next most important room in the rental property—the bathroom."

The Coach looked over to Brian as he spoke.

"Bathrooms can get dated very quickly, and because they are such 'personal' places, they need to be appealing as well as functional."

Brian nodded; he had been planning to give their bathroom a work-over for ages but never quite got around to doing anything about it. It had, he knew, become something of a sore point with Sarah. Being careful to avoid eye contact with her, he cleared his throat and asked, "How does this compare with the kitchen, Coach?"

"They are both rooms in which a lot of time is spent, so you need to pay a lot of attention to getting them right. Bathrooms are slightly less costly to renovate. Make sure the shower is enticing; replace the shower curtains or any cracked or dated glass doors. Fixtures should be updated and mirrors with cracks or faded silver need to be replaced. The bath tub can also be inexpensively relined if needed. And don't forget the floor. Retile if the existing tiles are in bad shape. Sometimes all it takes is to lay new tiles over the existing ones to make the floor look modern. Cabinets and towel rails are also easily and cheaply replaced."

Sarah continued with her notes and was quite content to leave the questions to Brian.

"Is it worthwhile getting a plumber in to look at the taps and plumbing, Coach?" he asked.

"If you need to, Brian. You can always replace fixtures or simple worn washers yourself, but new pipes are another matter. Remember again to stick within budget. Also remember to install an exhaust and heat light to update the room."

Bathrooms—
The second most important room for rental value
and time is the bathroom. Usually a complete
refit is called for, but again, budget is key.

"When it comes to the other rooms, be careful not to go overboard," the Coach continued.

"Sure it's nice to have great bedrooms, but the reality is that these aren't as important—from a real estate investment point of view—as the kitchen or bathroom. So do the minimum here. Paint the walls if they need it, update the light fixtures. See if you can get away with cleaning the carpets instead of replacing them. If not, then replace them, but watch your budget. I usually use an industrial-strength carpet."

Sarah looked puzzled; she wasn't convinced about the need to minimize here.

"Is this the real reason not to renovate the other rooms to the same standard as the kitchen or bathroom, Coach, or is there something else?" she asked.

"It all comes down to the cost, Sarah. Remember, you will have only allocated around 10 percent of the purchase price for renovation work, and you'll find that most of this will be consumed by the kitchen and bathroom. It's all a matter of containing costs so you can make a good return from your investment."

Other Rooms—
Don't go overboard on the rest of the house;
a coat of paint, new lighting, and new carpets
are usually all that's needed.

"It does pay to bear in mind that some things like floors, light fixtures, and other items that are hard working and subject to wear and tear should be brought up to snuff using industrial-grade materials because they need to last at least 10 years. Avoid the temptation to cut corners here; buy well and you'll save in the long run."

"I can relate to that, Coach," Brian said. He had always been a firm believer in investing in quality.

"And remember that although it may cost a little more, the cost is a tax deduction," the Coach added.

"So make sure you get a good appraisal done when you carry out the renovations because you need to get good figures to back up your claim for deductions and depreciation. Get this right and it will help reduce the actual cost to you with the added benefit that the job will last a long time, thus saving you money in the long run."

> **Lights, Floors, and Other Items—**
> **Remember, everything has to last at least 10 years, so go**
> **for industrial strength first and looks second. Remember**
> **to get appraisals for deductibility and depreciation.**

Sarah was getting the idea. She could already picture herself weighing up different properties to gauge their potential and what she should offer to make the deal attractive to her.

She understood perfectly why a budget of only 10 percent needed to be set aside for renovations, what type of renovations should be considered, and that sometimes things would have to be left as is to fit within their budget. She also understood which property renovations were to be avoided, but could think of at least two occasions when she wasn't quite sure what she should do.

"Coach, would there be times when we would be able to undertake more extensive renovations and still comply with your rules?" she asked.

"Sure, Sarah. You may need to take out a wall to open up a room, for instance," the Coach replied.

"You may also want to make a window bigger to take advantage of a view or a new deck you've just had built. Opening up a room can make a huge difference in the property without breaking the bank. It can also make a huge difference in the amount of rent you get."

"Think about this: it costs more to build a wall than it does to remove one, and many older homes are very closed in. How can you bring more light, more air, and generally more space to a property? One of my favorite things to do, in case you hadn't guessed, is to remove windows and put in bifold doors. They add great appeal and value."

> **Opening It Up—**
> **Taking out walls and making windows bigger is often a**
> **winner, especially if you can turn a back window into**
> **sliding or bifold doors to a new deck.**

"One of the easiest ways to add a whole lot to your new investment property's value and rental appeal is to mow the lawn, trim the hedges, and plant some new flowering annuals and shrubs," the Coach explained.

"Once you start looking at properties for sale, you'll be amazed at how many of them have no garden to speak of. I always find this strange because the garden is always the first thing people see, and first impressions do count. Adding a water feature, having a little landscaping done, or changing the character of an ordinary garden can work wonders and add thousands to the value at the same time.

"A lot of the time I rip out everything but the big trees and start again, with new lawns, new gardens with edges, and most importantly new fencing, or at least covering the inside of the older back fences."

"Coach, I've seen a lot of TV shows on this; they often do it with very low budgets as well," Brian added.

"Absolutely. The garden can be one area you do on your own. Sometimes, if you approach them right, neighbors will help pay for replacing old fences, and you don't have to use the most expensive or biggest plants; just make it easy to maintain."

Gardens and Outdoors—
Here's where a little money can go a very long
way to increase your rental income and overall value.
First impressions say it all; a clean and fresh garden
can add thousands to any property.

"But, Coach, surely there are times when we'd want to do something a little more extensive like adding an extra room or converting the garage into a family room," Sarah observed.

This was something she and Brian had been toying with years ago but never got around to. And now that their family had all but grown up, she was glad they didn't. Yet she could envisage situations where this kind of renovation could be desirable, particularly now that they were about to become property investors.

"There may be cases where this is simple to do, Sarah, and in such cases, it can make a really huge difference to the rentals you receive as well as the overall value of the property. However, you do need to be careful because this is more than just a facelift. It's a whole new ball game. You really need to be certain about your numbers and what it will do for you as far as your overall goals and objectives are concerned.

"Remember, when you go from giving a property a cosmetic facelift to a building job, you have everything from applications and permits to contractors and timings to take care of. It's often very worthwhile, but it also increases your workload. I would suggest that as you gain more experience you will be able to do a whole lot more of this."

Changing Structure—
Adding an extra bedroom or bathroom can be a solid
change that makes a massive difference to rentals and
therefore values. Remember that this is more than just a
facelift. Now you're into serious number crunching.

"While we're looking at some of the more major things you can do while renovating," the Coach continued, "I'd like to touch on a strategy that can make you good money. Buying well is still paramount, but you need to be able to see what others can't."

Sarah was writing furiously now, but still found time to squeeze in a quick question.

"What type of things do you have in mind, Coach?" she asked and almost immediately wished she hadn't. It was, she decided, rather obvious, and here she was making herself look as if she hadn't learned much since their coaching had begun.

"The sorts of things you might want to do here include converting a large house into room-by-room student accommodation, converting a block of units into Strata or Unit Title units, buying apartments and adding another floor or courtyard to increase rentable space, changing the floor plan of a block of units, or changing a purpose-built warehouse or even squash courts into apartments or units.

"I don't really want you trying things this adventurous first time out, but I want you to have them in the back of your mind, so you know to learn as much as you can as you are doing your simpler first few investments."

Sarah sighed; the Coach never ceased to surprise her. She completed her notes, put down her pen, and leaned back in her seat. She sensed the session was coming to an end. It had been another good one.

"Next week we will be discussing buying your first investment property," the Coach said. "This is where the fun starts."

Brian smiled. He wasn't sure whether it was a nervous smile or one of excitement. Either way he was sure they would be in for something memorable.

They thanked the Coach for the session, gathered up their possessions, and bade him farewell.

"Until next week," he said, waving as they made their way to their car.

Changing Use—
Changing the property from a house that's rented into rooms for rent or even two apartments can give me a great return. As I get more experience, it's time to really put my renovation hat on and rebuild so I can get more rental and therefore more value.

Part 9

■ Buy Where You Are an Expert—50, 10, 3, 1

Sarah knew they would be soon taking their first tentative steps towards becoming real estate investors. She also knew that, because they had a Coach, things would go a whole lot smoother than otherwise would have been the case.

Brian kept remarking on how much they had learned over the past few months. He said he was certain that taking the time and effort to learn as much as they could would stand them in good stead when the time came for them to get serious and start the hunt for their first investment property.

They both could feel the excitement growing on a daily basis. Brian had noticed that whenever Sarah picked up the Saturday newspaper, she now always flipped straight through to the real estate section first.

How their lives had already changed, he thought. And he wondered at how they would change further once they got the ball rolling and began getting serious about investing in their future.

As the day for their next coaching session drew nearer, Brian found himself wondering whether he would actually be up to it; he wondered whether those familiar stomach pains would reoccur.

This question remained at the forefront of his mind as he drove the now familiar route from their home to the Coach's office, found a parking spot, and switched the ignition off. He thought he detected a slight sigh of relief from Sarah, but decided not to probe further; he silently cursed himself for remaining unusually quiet on the road.

Sarah knew there would be much occupying her husband's mind and decided to leave things be. There would be more than enough time to talk and discuss their plans shortly. This was, she sensed, the calm before the storm.

"Hello, folks," the Coach said as he opened the door and invited them in. "How has the past week been?"

"I'd have to say it's been an emotional roller coaster, Coach," Brian replied.

"Really? Tell me more."

"No, it's nothing serious," Brian corrected himself. "I guess the anticipation is growing, and we can't wait to put into practice what we have been learning."

They took their seats.

"I suppose you could say that the learning is only just beginning, Brian," the Coach replied.

"See, the hard work is just about to begin. When you get out there to start looking for your first property—and those that will surely follow—there is really no substitute for hard work. It really does take a lot of effort to become successful at this game; if it didn't, everyone would be doing it. Most of the work I am talking about here is physically getting out and about and inspecting properties, talking to agents and other knowledgeable people, and gathering enough information to allow you to make informed decisions."

Brian nodded. He wasn't afraid of hard work. Besides, he had long been looking for something like this that he could get passionate about.

"The good thing about real estate is that once you have learned something, you know it forever. You won't have to keep relearning how to succeed in real estate. The principles remain the same; all you need to do is to get out there and gather the right information to enable you to invest wisely and according to your plans. The first one will be the hardest; from there it gets easier and easier."

Do the Work—
It takes effort to become an expert in real estate investing,
but remember you only have to learn things once.

"There really is no substitute for doing the work in this game," the Coach continued. "If you take shortcuts and try to get away without doing the legwork, you will ultimately pay the price."

Sarah nodded as she wrote.

"If you don't gather enough information about the current state of your chosen marketplace, how will you know whether it is a rising or falling market? How will you know what rental demands are doing? How will you know whether rents themselves are rising or falling? And how will you know whether you have a good deal or not? Is your mortgage rate the best it could be, and should you be locking in to a fixed rate or a variable one? If you don't do your homework well here, you will stand no chance of making the best decisions possible, will you?"

Sarah again nodded.

"Remember, mistakes made in this game are very costly. Most people can't afford to make mistakes and those who can, needn't; it's like throwing money away.

"What's another way people can be lazy in real estate investing, team?" the Coach questioned.

"By only seeing one realtor, or a couple of properties, or just one suburb, Coach," Brian was first to respond.

Sarah then jumped in, "Or they can simply go to a seminar where they sell properties and not go looking on their own. They could take someone else's word that it's a good deal."

"Excellent work, team. You got all the big ones," the Coach gave them yet another page for their notes.

Lazy Equals Paying Too Much—
If I take shortcuts, I will pay the price. Remember, lazy
people pay too much and don't make good returns.
It's worth doing the work.

"This is where we are going to start getting practical," the Coach began. "So make notes because tomorrow I am going to want you to start getting out and looking at more properties."

Brian felt his heart flutter. This is it, he thought.

"I want you to cast your net widely; I want you to look at no less than 50 properties."

Brian whistled in surprise.

"So many, Coach?" That seemed to him to be a little much.

Sarah had an open mind, but she also wondered at this.

"Why is it important to look at 50 properties, Coach?" asked Brian.

Sarah too couldn't contain herself and quickly added, "And how long is that going to take?"

The Coach could tell this was something that had taken them both by surprise. That didn't bother him; in fact he welcomed it because it meant they were involved.

"Well, you can actually easily do it in a weekend," he responded.

"But here's a tip. Get yourself a reasonable digital camera or camera phone and take photos of each place. That way you will be able to remember them when you get back home that night. I download them into a special file in my computer. I would also recommend that you invest in a copy of your local area map or guide, on disc if possible, as you'll find it invaluable when it comes to considering the properties. It will show you the area, where the facilities are, and where negative factors like municipal dumps or industrial areas are."

Brian nodded, satisfied. Sarah smiled at him, knowing they could now move on.

"Now it's time to consider how to apply some of this theory to the game of investing in real estate."

Sarah rubbed her hands together in anticipation. This was the part she was looking forward to most.

"Sourcing properties will be the first activity you need to get involved in," the Coach began.

"You first need to develop a list of suitable properties to consider. You will then use your rules and criteria to decide which of these make it onto your short list and which don't."

"So how do we do this, Coach? Where do we start?" she asked.

"The first thing you must do, Sarah, is to visit real estate agents in the area or areas you want to target. Get to know them. Ask them what stock they have on their books. Keep in touch with them. Phone them every week, as most won't keep in touch with you. Get to know everything about your area—the professionals call it farming your area."

"What if we don't have the time to do all this?" she asked.

"You could then make use of buyer's agents. They work on behalf of buyers and, for a fee of around 2 to 2½ percent, they'll do all the legwork as well as the negotiations for you."

Sarah nodded and made a few notes.

"So how else can you source properties?" the Coach prodded.

When he could see that he wasn't going to get a response, he continued: "Local newspapers are another excellent source. Not only will they tell you what is on the market at the time, they'll also inform you of trends, buying and selling patterns, and future market expectations."

The Coach gave them a few moments to make notes, and then asked: "Who else could you use?"

After a few more moments of silence he continued: "Rental managers are another excellent source that are generally overlooked. You see, there are real estate businesses that handle only rental investment properties. They don't sell property at all. If you keep close to them, the time will come—and it frequently does—when an owner wants to sell for whatever reason. They inform the Rental Managers of their intentions. Now if those managers knew you were in the market, they would advise the owner that they could already have a buyer. This would save them the trouble, and expense, of putting it on the market with a traditional real estate agent. And because you will probably want to keep the property as a rental, you'd be requiring a Rental Manager anyway, so offer to leave the property with them. They do, after all, know the place and its history."

Brian liked that suggestion; he always found himself attracted to the more unconventional ways of doing things.

"Property managers are another great source, as they are generally among the first to know when a unit is about to come on the market. And if they knew they would get a quick turnaround of owners of a unit, it would be in their interests to work with you, wouldn't it?"

Sarah nodded.

"Many newspaper and real estate company Web sites have an e-mail notification service where you can enter your desired property details, and whenever a property comes on the market that matches your preselected criteria, an e-mail is generated and sent to you. Make use of modern technology as much as possible, as it will make your task of inspecting 50 properties that much easier."

The Coach cleared his throat and reached for his glass of water.

"You'll need to develop a good database as you go, and keep good records. You don't want to keep phoning up the same person, especially if he is an owner of a property that might be on the rental market. You need to know who you've been in touch with, about which properties, and what the outcome was. You'll be surprised at how confusing this can become once you start working a few areas."

Brian looked up and asked, "Any advice about what to do and what not to do when we get started, Coach?"

"My advice is not to get too carried away. Hang on to your income but invest your time doing market research. Drive home using different routes each day to get a feel for what's going on in the area. Phone agents, and get knowledgeable. Farm your area; that way, agents will treat you seriously."

Sarah smiled; this was the type of stuff she wanted to grasp.

"Keep records on the rental market in your chosen area. When you get a sniff that a property you find suitable may be coming on the market, phone the owners to see if they would be interested in selling. If they are, even remotely, get face-to-face as soon as possible, because if you don't you could lose out because the owner would probably contact the local real estate agent for an opinion on what it might be worth. If this should happen, the agent will be pushing for an agency agreement, and if they're successful, it will mean a more difficult negotiation for you and most probably a higher sale price. You do need to act very quickly if you ever get a hint that an owner might be interested in selling."

Sarah had some reservations because she was not the extrovert who could easily do this.

"Isn't that a little overwhelming for someone like me, Coach? I mean, I am not at all comfortable about doing this. In fact, just the thought of it frightens me. But if you say it is a strategy I should seriously consider, how can I maximize my chances of not making a mess of it?"

"Develop a script, and use it," the Coach responded.

"Jot down all the possible objections an owner may throw at you, and think of responses you'd use to counter them. Refine your script as you go, making additions and corrections from the experience you gain talking to owners and agents. Practice on your family and friends before you get out in the marketplace. The more you do it, the better it will get. You'll find it an invaluable tool."

The Coach leaned across his desk, picked up two handouts, and passed them to his clients.

"This page is a really good evaluation form that I recommend you use when working your way through your 50 properties. This will help you when you get out and about."

Sarah looked at her handout for a moment, then slid it into the back of her notebook. She would study it later.

"That's it for today, folks," the Coach said as he stood and began making his way from behind his desk towards his clients.

"Between now and when we next meet, I want you to make a concerted effort to look at 50 properties. But just look; don't make any offers yet. The idea is to gather all the information you'll need to start making offers. But we'll talk about that next week.

"Also, make 50 copies of the handout and fill one out for every property you go see."

They said their good-byes to the Coach and thanked him for the session. The game was now well and truly on.

Look at 50—
To really get a good idea of what the market is doing, I need to look at at least 50 properties in a given suburb and complete the evaluation form for every one.

Property Evaluator   Rating A B C

Source _____	Agency _____
Asking Price $ _____	Address _____
Property Address _____	Address _____
	Salesperson _____
Suburb _____ UBD Ref ____	Phone _____
Position _____	Mobile _____

Aspect _____ Situation _____

Comments _____

Type   Units / Flats / House / Split Block / Redevelopment Site / Subdivision / V Land
Construction   Cav Brick / Brick Veneer / Timber / Fibro / Other _____**Finish**_____
Roof   Terra Cotta Tile / Concrete Tile / Iron / Fibro / Other   **Floor**   Timber / Concrete
Linings Solid Plaster / Whiteset / Exposed Brick / Paster Board / Fibro / Other _____
Overall Condition _____
Land Area _____ **Zoning** _____ **Age** ____ **Building Size** ____ **Bedrooms** __
Car Accomodation __ Lock up / __ Carport / ___ Other **Laundry** ____ **Bathrooms** __
Services   Gas / Elec / Phone / Water / Sewer / Septic / Cable
Transport   Train _____ Bus_____ Ferry _____ Other _____

Why Property for Sale _____

Previous Offers _____ Date _____ Time on Market _____

		Renovation Calculator		
Rental Income	$ _____	**Strip and Clean**		$ _____
Rates	$ _____	Plaster	m x $	$ _____
Insurance	$ _____	Plumbing	m x $	$ _____
Body Corp Fees	$ _____	Electrical		$ _____
Management Fees	$ _____	Wetseal	m x $	$ _____
Other	$ _____	Paint	m x $	$ _____
Ratio (Rent:Price)	_____	Kitchen	m x $	$ _____
Rent Movement	$ _____	Laundry		$ _____
Purchase Price	$ _____	Garage		$ _____
Deposit	$ _____	Tiling	m x $	$ _____
PIA Report ROI	_____ %	Carpet	m x $	$ _____
Repayments	$ _____	Blinds	x $	$ _____
		Stoves		$ _____
Cash Flow Positive / Neutral / Negative		Hot Plates		$ _____
Amount $ _____ P/W $ _____ P/A		Range Hood		$ _____
		Dishwasher		$ _____
		Sink		$ _____
		Tapware		$ _____
		Shower Screen		$ _____
		Screens		$ _____
		Sundry		$ _____
		Total		$ _____

Assessment

Investment / Speculative / H B S

Buy & Hold	Quick Cash	Cashflow
Long Term	Time Frame	Value
Short Term	__ Mths	$_____

Proceed / Hold / Forward date   ___ / ___ / ___

The week had flown by, and before Brian knew it, it was time again for their weekly coaching session.

He felt as if his head were swimming; it had been such a tumultuous week, yet it had also been a fulfilling one. In fact, he had remarked to Sarah as they climbed back into their car and headed for the Coach's office that he couldn't remember when last he had had so much fun.

Sarah agreed. She too had really enjoyed the experience. She had earlier confided in Brian that she wasn't really looking forward to it, but once they got into the swing of things, it turned out to be far easier and less stressful than she had imagined.

They had followed the Coach's advice to the letter. Sarah really enjoyed constructing files on the computer to store and organize all the notes, comments, photos, and general information regarding the 50 properties they had looked closely at.

"Boy, you were right, Coach," she said as they took their seats in his office.

"We couldn't possibly have remembered anything about particular properties after we had seen five or six. My head was soon swimming with information. I would have gone into information overload within hours had we not equipped ourselves like you suggested."

"So you got through 50?" he asked.

"You bet," Brian replied, his heart swelling with pride at the smile on the Coach's face.

"Well done, you are off to a flying start! Didn't you find that you quickly got a very good grip on the market? I'm sure you began very soon to feel what was good value and what wasn't."

"You're not wrong there, Coach," Brian replied. "I was amazed at how quickly this happened. I think we now have a very good feel for what is happening in the market and we have been able to identify some very good prospects."

"That's fantastic. So let's talk now about selecting properties to put offers in on."

Sarah was excited. This is what she had been waiting for.

"So, is there an art to selecting the right property?" she asked.

"No, not really," the Coach replied. "I recommend you develop a check sheet that reminds you what your rules are and what specifically you are looking for. Like anything else, investing in real estate can be anything but smooth sailing. Some investors seem to make just about every mistake in the book. Others seem to succeed despite themselves, benefiting more from being in the right place at the right time. In reality, these people are not really investors at all. They're better described as speculators.

"Serious investors always takes a planned approach to investing in real estate. And so they should because it is, after all, a serious business. That doesn't mean it needn't be fun. In fact I believe it should be."

Sarah nodded.

"You need to follow a carefully planned and well-thought-out strategy based on a set of rules to ensure that your chances of making costly mistakes are minimized. Why learn the hard way? Why not heed what others have done before you by taking note of what works and what doesn't?"

This made perfect sense to Sarah, and she knew Brian would be thinking so too.

"Could you run through a few of the more common pitfalls that lie in wait for the unwary investor?" Sarah asked.

"Sure. After years of experience in the real estate market, I've seen investors at all levels continually making the same basic mistakes," the Coach explained.

"There are certain basic pitfalls that snare even some of the more astute and experienced investors. The good news is they're simple mistakes that are easily avoided. All that's required is a basic awareness of them. They include overcapitalization, thinking you're smarter than you actually are, not understanding your market, cost blowouts when renovating, time blowouts when renovating, not having a check sheet, pest inspection certificates that don't indicate whether previous pest damage has been rectified, and lastly, not including sufficient clauses on contracts."

Sarah again thanked her lucky stars for being able to write in shorthand.

"When you begin looking for the approximately 10 properties you are now going to make offers on, you need to base your decision on factors that would rule out unsuitable properties. You need to be able to recognize what kind of property to avoid, not because it may be a bad house, but because it doesn't meet your particular needs or rules at the time. You must be able to recognize something that doesn't fit with your game plan."

Sarah knew exactly what the Coach was talking about, as she was already ruling out some of the 50 houses they had looked at by using this strategy.

"As a general rule, I would advise you to stay well clear of properties that fall into the categories listed on this handout."

He picked up his folder, took two sheets of paper from it and handed them over to Sarah.

• A house you think you might live in at some point. It could be a house on the coast that you think you should buy now and move into when you eventually retire. Don't make the mistake of confusing lifestyle decisions with investment decisions. By all means buy yourself a retirement cottage at the coast—only don't include it with your investment properties.

• Properties being marketed by people who buy the property at one price and sell it to you at an inflated value that bears no relevance to its real market value, only to the fact that they have very good sales machines. These types of deals have received considerable negative publicity, and are best avoided.

They are usually easily identified by the agent's promise to fly you interstate to view the property at no cost to yourself.

• Anything where you have to pay full price. By this I do not mean you should never pay the asking price. Understand that if you are after a top-quality property in a top location, you may have to pay a reasonable amount for it. That's the reality. It's simply a question of supply and demand. But I believe these instances will be fairly few and far between. Discount is king!

• A property you fall in love with—unless you're going to live there a *long* time. Remember what I said about not letting your emotions get in the way of a good deal?

• Anything that puts you into so much debt you can't sleep at night.

• A lot of building value and very little dirt value. The real value in owning real estate isn't so much the value of the building (which depreciates over time) but the value of the land (which increases over time). I very seldom hold units long-term for this reason unless they are full blocks where I own the land as well.

• A lot of house value with no suburb or street value. It's often not rewarding owning the very best house in an average street or suburb.

• Anything where the numbers don't work. Otherwise, what's the point?

"Stick with your rules, follow these simple guidelines, and take it seriously. If you do this, then by the time you have inspected 50 properties, you will have identified around 10 that will be what you are after. Now it's simply a matter of sitting down with the agent and making offers on them."

Sarah looked up sharply.

"You mean we are to go and do this now?"

"Well, not right now. Wait until we have completed next week's session, which is all about how to negotiate," the Coach laughed.

"But make sure you have chosen 10 by next week, even if that means revisiting some of the properties. See you next week. And good luck."

Offers on 10 According to Your Rules—
Because I am working according to my rules, out of every
50 properties I look at, around 10 will meet my rules. And
as my offers are made based on my numbers, I know that
many will not be accepted. This is why I should aim at
submitting 10 offers for every 50 properties I see.

At the start of their next session, the Coach got right down to business.

"Remember, as long as you satisfy the seller's *real* reason for selling, they'll give on everything else, and often the price is the first casualty. It's human nature."

Sarah paused thoughtfully, sucked on the end of her pen, and asked, "What, in your experience, are the main reasons that motivate people to sell?"

"I have found there are usually six things that motivate vendors. I call them the Six Ds of Motivated Vendors:

- **Death**—Deceased estates are not nice but usually the relatives just want out.

- **Divorce**—They just want out of the relationship fast.

- **D' Bank**—They can't make repayments and need to sell now to recoup any equity they have.

- **Don't Know**—People who don't know how much their property is worth as they picked a price themselves.

- **Deadlines**—Anyone who has to sell by a certain date.

- **Developers**—They are running a business and can get stuck with a cashflow problem.

"These people are ready and waiting to give you a property at a very cheap price if you can find them and negotiate well."

Brian continued taking notes and left the discussion to his wife.

"You must have learned many good lessons over the years, Coach. Can you share some with us?"

"Sure. Lesson 1—Written Contracts Change Minds: Sellers' emotions are really hit hardest when a written contract of offer is in their hands. Somehow offers aren't real unless they are in writing sitting in front of you. It's easy to be macho when it's all talk, but much harder when it's on your table in black and white. When that happens, sellers' brains have strange things happen to them—they go all mushy. They have to make a decision then and there. It's just them, the real estate agent (who is only interested in the commission check), and the deal.

"Lesson 2—Time Erodes Certainty: This is a biggie. The more time you give sellers, the more negotiable they become and the more power you have. Time is your greatest weapon, so use it wisely.

"Lesson 3—Money in the Hand Is a Power Tool: A $100,000 check in your hand creates all sorts of emotions like: imagine what I could do with this—new car, better house, overseas trip. The mind goes wild dreaming and exploring all sorts of possibilities. Let me put it this way. If you were selling a property and had two offers, one with a deposit check and one without, which one would you take? I have used this tactic over and over again with amazing results. Now understand you won't get a strike every time, but you will get good results and often you'll surprise yourself. Was it worth my risking a $500 gift basket to turn a losing deal into a winning one? Absolutely!

"Lesson 4—Family Pressure Is Hard to Say No To: What do you think would have happened when the $500 gift basket I sent arrived? Everyone would have come running with comments like . . . 'Wow, that's cool; I want the chocolates,' 'Who sent it, Dad?' or 'You must have really been good to someone.' "

Sarah was intrigued.

"I am determined to become better at negotiating, Coach. Can you give me any tips that will help me do this?"

"Yes. I would suggest you read up all you can on Neuro-Linguistic Programming, or NLP for short."

"What's that?" she responded.

"NLP is a model of human behavior and communication that draws from the knowledge of psychodynamics and behavioral theories," the Coach continued.

"It is concerned with the identification of patterns in our communication and behavior and how we interact in the process of change."

"So what does this mean for negotiating?" she asked.

"If we can understand the key components of NLP, we can become better negotiators. We don't have time to go into details, as it's a huge subject, but I recommend you read up as much as you can.

Sarah was again itching to get something off her chest.

"Let's get back to the subject of empathy, if you don't mind, Coach," she said. "I really do believe that this is very important."

"Good point, Sarah. It certainly is vital. Look around for clues. Pick up on things that are important to the sellers. Look for, and understand, what it is they cherish. Let me give you an example.

"When I walk into a place, the first thing I always say is, 'This is incredible! I wasn't expecting anything like this. I just love that main road out front.' Where does that leave the seller? He would probably have been dreading overcoming objections to the main road, and would have no room for maneuvering. You see, his whole negotiating strategy would have been developed to deal with it as an issue, and now it would have been turned upside down. This leaves him with only one thing left to talk about—the price. This brings us back to the basics. Remember what I said about the different perceptions buyers and sellers have about the selling process? Sellers sell on value, but buyers buy on price. You need to get them firmly away from the 'value' plane and place them squarely in the 'price' plane. This is your territory. It's where you call the shots. You are in charge of the encounter. Of course, when you're selling, you'll be aiming to get the buyer all emotionally involved, as this is 'value' territory."

Brian was impressed. He liked the idea of taking unusual approaches, especially when it didn't involve intimidating the other party.

"That's a great strategy, Coach. Any other pearls of wisdom?" he asked.

"Well, often you don't actually get to meet the owner, but over the years I've learned that a way to interact with the seller directly is to drop back in about an hour or so after your inspection with the realtor. You can tell the seller that you're truly interested and that you just wanted to see the bathroom again, that you couldn't remember whether it was blue or green.

"That way you get to meet them and start talking about why they are selling, why you want to buy, and you can even strike a deal and then both drive to the realtors and ask them to draw up the paperwork for you."

Brian smiled in amazement. "I'll bet the realtors would love to have a deal become that easy for them to get their commission, Coach."

"They sure do. I've never met one who wasn't happy to have a deal that she just has to write the paperwork on. I'm also a real fan of creative financing that turns good deals into exceptional ones," the Coach continued. "You are only limited by the possibilities your mind can come up with."

As Sarah finished taking notes, she looked up, thought for a moment, and then asked, "You'll have guessed by now that even the thought of entering into negotiations scares me. But this is something I really want to overcome. Now I know you have rules for just about everything, Coach, so are there any you have about negotiating?"

The Coach smiled, as he was glad Sarah wanted to push through her boundaries. "There are a few rules I have when negotiating deals that I *never* break. First, I never submit an unconditional cash offer unless the seller is under massive time pressure to sell by a deadline. In this case I do my due diligence first, give him a low unconditional cash offer with a time limit of say 24 hours and, in the odd case, attach a nice healthy deposit check."

"Why would you never submit an unconditional cash offer, Coach?" she asked with a puzzled look on her face. "I would have thought that would have given you a great bargaining advantage."

"The reason I never do so, unless the circumstances I've just mentioned present themselves, is because it leaves me no room to negotiate. The conditions must be right and the offer must be really great."

Sarah understood. There was more to this business than at first met the eye, she decided.

"I rarely attend an auction because that way I can have a realtor or friend bid for me up to my predetermined limit," the Coach continued. "I find auctions tougher because I have to spend money to conduct the necessary pest and building inspections or any other due diligence checks before I even know if I have a deal."

Sarah had always been very wary of auctions and was glad to hear this.

"Auctions shift the power from the buyer to the seller, and I don't really like being involved in any process I don't control," the Coach went on.

"Be aware that you are still in the negotiation phase of the process until the deal becomes unconditional and all the clauses that your offer was subject to become fulfilled. And always include conditions in every offer."

"What kinds of conditions, Coach?" Sarah asked.

"Some of the favorite clauses I use are Due Diligence Clauses, Partners Approval Clauses, Appropriate Finance Clauses, Access Clauses, Facsimile Clauses, Vendor Finance Clauses, and Renovation and Improvements Clauses."

"Why do you use them?" Sarah continued.

"I use clauses to protect and safeguard me in the negotiation and it provides a lever where I can buy extra time if I need to. Here's what I mean:

"Suppose I came across this solid deal that I knew would sell like hotcakes. Let's also suppose it's one of those deals that I need to do right away or I'll lose it. How do I buy myself enough time to 'do the numbers'?"

Sarah responded as quick as a flash: "Use a few clauses."

"I explain to the seller that I really love the place, and I'm quite happy to put forward a cash contract for the asking price, but I really can't make such a decision without first showing the property to my wife," the Coach explained. "Now as she's out of town and won't be back for another week, I'm more than happy to submit a cash offer, subject only to my wife seeing the place and agreeing to the purchase within seven days. Very few sellers will pass up an offer like that."

"So what is the effect of doing this?" Sarah asked.

"This takes the property off the market, giving me time to run through my figures and carry out the necessary checks. If the deal doesn't stack up, I can still pull out simply by having my wife reject the deal. Oh, and it's a good idea to actually have a wife, otherwise legally you may have a hard time getting out of the contract," the Coach laughed. "A partner or business partner works equally well."

The session had flown—a sure sign that both Brian and Sarah had found it extremely useful and interesting. On their way out, they thanked the Coach and took their handout.

Negotiate on Three—
If I submit 10 offers based on my numbers, I will be
able to aim at negotiating on 3 of them. Most of my offers
will get a counteroffer rather than a yes or no.

Brian had been looking forward to the session on finance for ages; he knew the importance of finding the right financial package, especially for someone like him who didn't have spare cash lying around. In fact, all he really had was equity in the family home, and he sometimes even struggled to make ends meet.

Sarah really didn't know too much about their finances; she had always left it all to Brian. Yet she found herself really looking forward to the session, partly because anything the Coach spoke about she found fascinating, but also because she had come to realize during the coaching sessions that she was more capable than she had always given herself credit for.

They found themselves leaving home and heading for the Coach's office slightly earlier than usual, such was their enthusiasm. Brian had remarked about this and they both agreed it was probably due more to the fact that they really loved learning about investing in the real estate market than the topic of that session. They also knew the course was nearing an end and they would really begin testing the saying that the proof of the pudding was in the eating.

"There are many ways to finance your deals," the Coach began as soon as the usual pleasantries had been dispensed with. "Some of them are obvious; others aren't."

Brian opened his notepad and began writing.

"Which type you choose largely depends on you," the Coach continued. "But if you're not smart about this, you could end up like most investors and only ever own one or two investment properties.

"You need to apply a large measure of lateral thinking here, because if you can't finance a deal, it's no deal. You can make all the offers you like, but unless you can come up with the money, you're wasting your time."

"So how do we go about this, Coach?" Brian asked. "How do we finance a deal?"

"The simple answer is any way you can," the Coach responded. "Consider all your options. Here I am talking about the equity you may have in your own home, refinance options, and even, as you gain more experience, seller financing."

"Mmm, I hadn't thought of getting the sellers to loan me the money to buy their property, Coach," Brian said.

"Make your home work for you. It's probably the cheapest money you'll ever come across. The question you need to ask is how much could the equity in your home be earning you right now? Unless you're using it to purchase other property, the answer is none!"

"Refinancing an existing property is another great method for raising money. I use one of the following four strategies when doing a deal so I can refinance the property within six months and get my money back: buy, renovate, and refinance; buy at a discount and refinance; buy and change the property's use and refinance; and buy in a high capital growth area, ride the property value up, and then refinance. Each of these options will work; it's just the time frames that change."

"Seller financing is not commonly used, but it's a great finance option and I have personally done numerous such deals. Simply put, the sellers sell the property to you for say $300,000 and they agree to finance $50,000 of the purchase price at 7.5 percent for 12 months. This means you have a sale contract for $300,000 on which just about any bank will loan you 80 percent ($240,000). This means you only need to come up with $10,000 to do the deal: settlement day: $250,000 required, bank mortgage: $240,000, amount required by you: $10,000."

Brian was intrigued.

"Why would people want to finance a property they were selling, Coach?" he asked. "Surely the reason they were selling was to make money?"

"There are many sellers who do not have an immediate need for all of the proceeds of the sale of a property," the Coach explained. "They may be retired people, financially independent, or have other reasons. Nevertheless, they may be willing to leave in a portion of the purchase price (say 10 percent or 20 percent) for a one- or two-year period. If you can provide a genuine reason for needing the finance, such as 'I have the extra $20,000, but I want to invest it in renovations and cosmetic improvements to the property to maximize its value,' then a seller will often be prepared to assist you."

"But, Coach, how do the banks feel about deals like this?" Brian asked.

"The bank is very happy for you to use other people's money for financing when you are more experienced. Generally because they are still first on the list with security over the title," the Coach responded. "The best use of seller financing is on sellers who are either motivated vendors—the Six Ds—or have made substantial profit on the property and are prepared to finance a purchaser into a property so they can realize some of their profit immediately and some over time."

Brian nodded, seeing the sense in the argument.

"What other strategies have you used to finance the deal, Coach?" he asked. "I somehow know you have some real beauties up your sleeve."

"In fact there are another three," he replied. "Let's start with subsidized deposit or vendor gifting. This is similar to seller financing, but it involves the seller giving you a discount for an early settlement. This is normally a separate agreement than the sale agreement and can have some nasty tax implications for the seller if not structured correctly. Again, these strategies are primarily for you once you gain more experience, but I just want you to be open to the ideas as you learn.

"Then there are personal loans. Don't overlook them. They are most useful for paying for things like deposits, refurbishments, and renovations. Most banks have a facility to give personal loans to their customers, so make inquiries.

"Credit cards are another great way to finance deposits, refurbishments, or renovations. Many successful investors use their 55-day interest-free credit cards for their quick cash deals, knowing they will have sold the property by the time the money is fully due."

Brian was impressed. He hadn't thought of the credit card, even though he had two and used them regularly. Sarah was always telling him he had come to rely on them.

"There are many institutions that will advance you the money to finance your real estate deals," the Coach went on. "Apart from the major banks, there is a whole raft of second-tier lenders who aggressively chase new business. I deal with a wide range of them and am very satisfied with the results. Of course, some of the deals I did to get started did involve higher-than-normal interest rates, high establishment fees, and early exit penalties.

"My point here is that I don't particularly care about these things, as long as I know about them when I do the deal. You see, if I factor them into my calculations and I still make a profit, that's fine. I don't begrudge lenders their share of the profits if I achieve my objective with my deal. In many cases, I'm faced with the choice of making an acceptable profit or no profit at all. The fact that the lender makes a healthy profit as well doesn't really bother me."

Brian nodded; he had no argument with that line of reasoning.

"Let me give you another example of creative thinking when structuring a deal," the Coach said, looking this time at Sarah. He was mindful not to exclude her in this discussion.

"I recently negotiated a property that involved three two-bedroom vacation flats *and* a vacant block of land. The owner needed to sell. He was asking $440,000 for the lot. The units and vacation flat were returning him an income of around $41,000 a year.

"My offer was $350,000 for the units. And because the bank would only lend me 80 percent of the purchase price—that's $280,000—I wanted seller financing of $70,000 to cover the rest. This would mean I didn't have to outlay any money."

Brian nodded, following the logic.

"At first the vendor was skeptical, saying he was short of cash and would need to get a full-time job. But my calculations hinged on the assumption I wasn't going to outlay any capital. So I then played my trump card. In addition to the

$350,000 for the units—$280,000 from the bank and $70,000 vendor financed—I offered $160,000 for the vacant land with settlement in a year's time.

"This meant he'd achieve $510,000 for both the units and the land instead of his asking price of $440,000. The difference, I explained, being the $70,000 I was asking for as seller financing. And to clinch the deal, I explained this amount would be deducted from the payment for the land at the time of settlement, bringing the total figure back down to his original asking price. That way I'd get my 'no cash down' deal and he would get his asking price, plus he wouldn't have to find a full-time job."

Brian was impressed. "So the end result was a sweet deal that suited everyone," he chipped in.

"That's right, and I'm now planning on developing the vacant land."

Sarah finished writing; she was taking it all in with a great deal of interest, even though finance was never her strong point. There was one question she had. Since the session began she was dying to ask the Coach what he thought of tapping into the trust funds most lawyers held. She had understood this was possible but nobody she had come across before had known anything about it.

"Coach, I have heard through the grapevine that lawyers have trust funds that investors can use as a form of borrowing. Do you know anything about this, and have you used it before?"

"Funny you should mention this, Sarah. They certainly can be a good source of ready capital, particularly for the short term. Another source is other investors, but I'll only consider them under my terms. Most will generally want a say in how you run or structure your business affairs. This I'll never agree to. As long as they only want to inject funds and then reap a return at the end, that's fine. Nothing else. Most are just not worth the hassle."

"And what about family members?" Sarah asked.

"If you borrow from family members, make sure you have an agreement in place. This is important because as time goes by, people's needs change. And their recollection of what you originally agreed to often becomes colored or blurred.

Things can also go wrong or not turn out as you expected. No deal is airtight, so make sure you use your lawyer to document agreements and have robust commercial processes that protect everyone."

Brian now had a question.

"Any advice about dealing with the bank, Coach?"

The Coach thought for a while, then said, "Dealing with bankers or brokers can be a challenge for many investors, and yet it's one of the crucial aspects of investing to master. It does not matter how many deals you can negotiate if you cannot get the funding to purchase them. Before I go any further, though, bankers are by far the best financiers any property investor will come across. Even with everything and every option we just discussed, you can't go past a good banker to borrow your money."

He paused to let that sink in.

"As they say, 'When in Rome, do as the Romans do.' When dealing with bankers, act as the bankers act! I have found that the more you understand how bankers think and what they are looking for, the easier it is to get their approval for more of their money."

"What types of things do they take into account, Coach?" Brian asked.

"Banks have three questions they need answered when they lend to you: is their money safe, can they make a profit from lending to you, and will you be competent at managing their money?"

Sarah nodded; nothing startling there, she thought. All good common sense, but good to know.

"In the banking and mortgage lending business, there is a rule of thumb called 'The 4 Cs.' These are qualities banks want to see when they consider loaning you money. They are credit, capacity, collateral, and character."

Sarah was writing furiously now.

"Let's start with credit. A banker wants to determine that you are a good credit risk by seeing your current credit picture: a 'snapshot' of your past and present debt, current available credit, and a rating of your debt repayment history."

"Capacity is simply a measure of your financial capacity to repay the loan. This is measured by dividing your gross monthly income by the amount you are paying to service your total outstanding debts, including the new payment of the property you are planning to buy. Generally, bankers will allow up to 35 percent of your monthly income to be used for your housing or investment property expense *and* all other current obligations you have outstanding including credit cards, car loans, and student loans."

"Collateral is the valuation of the property you're about to purchase. The banker needs to know the value of the property you are 'pledging' as collateral for the loan."

"Character: Generally, to determine character, banks look at your job stability, your probability of continued employment, and the soundness of your financial habits."

"Remember, bankers are trained to look for the reason to say *no*, not *yes*. Banks will judge you on everything from your clothes to your proposal. Your proposal tells them how serious you are, and it gives them all the information they need to say yes."

"Can you give us any tips here, Coach?" Brian asked.

"Sure. Give them everything they need to say *yes!* Your financial presentation is everything. Never lie; you will eventually be found out, and you may find it difficult to get financing in the future with a black mark on your file. And spread your loans around more than one bank. That way if you need an extra $10,000, you'll find it easier to get $2000 unsecured from five banks than $10,000 from one bank.

"It's also good for asset protection and avoids one bank cross guaranteeing all mortgages with all properties, which can start a domino effect if you go through a difficult patch and the bank calls in some of their mortgages. And finally, your proposal should impress them and demonstrate your commitment. They love lots of figures, and so do their analysts."

Sarah put down her pen and asked, "Can you give us a quick rundown of the other costs that we need to allow for when we get to the stage of buying our first investment property, Coach?"

"There are a host of other costs you need to take into account when making an offer on a property," the Coach responded. "Factor them into your calculations. They may vary from region to region, but they will nevertheless form part of your transaction."

He picked up his glass of water and took a long drink.

"It's important to build in all the costs at this stage because the profit you make from buying and selling real estate is determined at the time you buy, not sell. Lock this into your brain and *never* forget it."

Sarah nodded and made a note.

"Here are some of the items you need to factor in:"

"**Legals.** I prefer a flat-rate deal with my legal team. And I pay slightly more than I have to because by doing so I know I'll build a good relationship with the firm in the long run. I also know that, while I might be paying a little more on cheaper properties, I'll be scoring on the expensive ones."

"**Stamp Duty or Transfer Tax.** This is unavoidable in most markets around the country and the rest of the world, unless you're buying a company. Let me explain. If you are buying a property that happens to be owned by a company, you might be better off buying the company. You see, it's a fairly common practice to set up an investment company purely to buy, and own, a large property. If you were to buy the company and the mortgage it has over the property, you'd pay only tax on the net asset and not the total value of the property. For example, if a company owned a property worth $1,000,000, but owed $800,000 on it, the company would be worth only $200,000. So, instead of paying transfer-type taxes or duties on the $1,000,000 property (as you would have to if you bought it in the usual manner), you'd pay only stamp duty on the $200,000 the company was worth. You could save even more if you were to approach the mortgagee with the request to release the previous company director's guarantee and substitute it with yours instead (presuming you were secure enough). This way the mortgage would also be transferred into your name, saving you the cost of rewriting the loan and other costs."

Brian was listening intently.

"A word of caution, though. When purchasing a company from another seller, have your lawyer complete a thorough due diligence to ensure that there are no hidden nasty company debts that are likely to come your way after the sale."

"**Valuation Fees.** Most financiers will want a property appraisal, so don't waste too much time and effort trying to avoid it. In fact, deliver it to them on a plate. He's what I do."

"Phone an appraiser (approved by your bank) and commission her to complete an appraisal for you. Supply the appraiser with all the supporting sales data (your local real estate agent will give you this), listing recent comparative house sales in the area, and tell the appraiser that you are still negotiating on the property but believe the property is worth X amount of dollars."

"Usually, the appraiser will then deliver you a valuation that is consistent with the amount you consider the property to be worth. Give this appraisal to the bank, and 95 percent of the time they will accept it without hesitation."

"**Loan Application Fees.** Try to get these waived, but first make sure there are no early pullout penalties."

"**Mortgage Insurance.** This is usually payable only if you want to get a mortgage that exceeds 80% of the value of the property. If you have a low deposit, consider this the cost of doing business."

"**Building Insurance.** I prefer arranging a blanket cover for all my properties. It's cheaper and more convenient this way than having a separate policy for each individual property. Negotiate bulk discounts whenever you can."

"**Contents Insurance.** I would recommend you include this in your building policy."

"**Agents' Fees.** There are none for buying properties unless you pay finder's fees or commissions to a buyer's agent. But you will have to pay agents' fees when you sell. These are also usually nonnegotiable."

"**Marketing Costs.** Most people fail to budget for this. When you do, it will make all the difference when the time comes to sell. You may want to consider placing a few color advertisements in the local newspapers, designing and printing a brochure (occasionally your real estate agent will provide these free of charge, so speak nicely to him), and erecting a large For Sale sign outside the property. There is a cost to effective marketing, but it's worth it for a quick sale. If you use a real estate agent to sell your property, she will facilitate getting all your marketing material produced, but you will usually have to pay for it.

"**Holding Costs.** These include items such as interest charges, mowing, and cleaning."

It was Sarah who now spoke: "So I guess the point is that most of these costs are unavoidable."

"That's right, Sarah, these costs are there and need to be covered. If you don't allow for them up front, they will come out of your profit."

It was time now for the session's handout. The Coach handed Sarah the sheet of paper, thanked them for their time, and confirmed details of their next session. Brian led Sarah to their parked car, opened the door for her, and then climbed in himself. It was another highly productive and successful session.

Finance One—
Of the three I negotiate, I will be able to finance and get a deal on usually just one. Not every banker will love every deal, but I give the bank a full proposal to make sure I give myself the best chance.

Part 10

I Build a Great Team

Sarah knew the time was fast approaching when they would be getting down to business and actually negotiating the purchase of their first investment property. Sure, they had already started laying the groundwork by getting out and inspecting properties. But until now they really felt as though there was no real commitment. Looking is cheap, she knew. And until now, they hadn't even gone so far as to write out a half-decent offer.

Or any other type of offer, for that matter.

She suddenly began to feel very vulnerable and all alone. She did have Brian on her side, she reminded herself. And the Coach. But somehow this didn't bring her much comfort. Brian would be in the same boat as she was, she knew, and the Coach, well, he was a great help and would always be, but how could she expect him to assist when they found themselves in the cut and thrust at the business end of the real estate game?

She had phoned the Coach during the week and raised this with him. He had told her not to worry, because the next session would be addressing this in detail.

This eased her mind considerably and she found herself, once again, looking forward to the next session.

"So now I want you to think about who will be playing the game with you," the Coach said as he began the session.

"Who will be on your team? Who will be playing the game with you?"

This excited Sarah; she began writing even before the Coach had finished speaking.

"Before you start negotiating seriously," the Coach explained, "you need to sit down and make a list of everyone who is part of your team. You need to understand who's on your side and who's not. Who will be helpful to have on your team? Who is essential? Make a list of all those you think you'll need."

Sarah nodded and said, "The first person I will need is a good real estate agent, Coach."

"Do you need just one on your team, Sarah? And are there good and bad Realtors if you're an investor?"

She looked up in surprise, but before she had a chance to reply, he continued.

"You see, if you walk into a real estate office and announce that you are interested in buying an investment property, many agents will show you houses with pretty gardens where the investment numbers are pathetic. It differs around the world, but about 80 percent of agents I've come across don't invest in property themselves; many wouldn't know what a hot property investment looks like if they tripped over it. You need to give them a feel for what you want to see."

"So, Coach, how do we pick the good ones?" Brian was a little worried.

"Brian, it's the helpful ones who turn into great agents; even the new agents can become a great help to you. What I do is interview them as if they were applying for a job while we are looking at the first one or two properties.

"Don't worry too much; the good ones will find their way to the top and the others will fall away. It's just like every other industry. So, how many do you think you'll need to get to know at the start?" The Coach turned it back to Brian and Sarah.

"A good few, so we'll probably meet a whole bunch and get to build relationships with a few who end up on our team." Sarah nodded as she spoke.

Sarah looked relieved. She had a friend who worked in real estate and was already thinking of the Realtors she'd met so far who could end up on their team.

Real Estate Brokers—
Great brokers or agents will save me both time and money.
I am going to find about 1 great agent for every 10 I deal
with. Eventually they will bring me deals rather than my
having to hunt for them.

"So, next on your team would be a great insurance agent. Insurance is a specialist field with a multitude of players in the market," the Coach continued.

"There are literally hundreds of different insurance packages out there, and finding the right one at the right price to suit your requirements takes more effort than it's worth. Let a good agent do this for you. And the best part is that it doesn't cost you anything, as the agent's fee comes as a commission from the insurance underwriters."

Sarah underlined a note in her book. She knew this must not be overlooked.

"So, Coach, are there certain traits we need to look for in a good agent?" Brian was leaning back in his chair pondering his own question.

"Well, you tell me, Brian. What do you think you should do to find a great agent?" Again the Coach made him think.

"Probably one who invests in real estate herself or at least has a lot of clients who invest already, Coach." Brian was pleased with his answer.

**Insurance Agents—
I have to insure everything, so having access to
a wide range of choices, and the best advice,
is crucial to my success as an investor.**

"Now, your average suburban lawyer just isn't good enough if you're aiming at investing in real estate in a big way," the Coach went on.

"Why is that, Coach?" Sarah asked. She had long since made a mental note of the lawyer they had used in the past at their local business center and had looked forward to the day she and Brian would walk in and ask for an appointment.

"You see, they are generalists," the Coach replied. "I believe you need to seek one who specializes in property law and property litigation. Again, go and interview a few to decide who should be on your team."

"So, Coach, should we use the criteria that they either invest or have a lot of clients who already do?" Sarah questioned.

"Absolutely."

Legal Eagles—
Drawing up great contracts and having someone
do the conveyancing or escrow efficiently, cost-effectively,
and quickly makes all the difference.

"So, on to accountants. The difference between a good one and a bad one can cost you thousands of dollars in lost tax deductions, and there is nothing sadder than lost tax deductions!"

"Again, interview and select your new team member."

He didn't need to explain any further; both Brian and Sarah knew precisely what he was getting at.

Accounting—
Keeping a finger on the financial pulse can save me
thousands, particularly as my portfolio expands.
An accountant who owns his own investment properties
will usually help me find all the deductions.

"As you accumulate investment properties, you'll also need a good property manager," the Coach explained.

"Why?" Sarah asked. She had heard of many who managed their own portfolios.

"Simply because they specialize in sourcing good tenants, conducting regular property inspections, and making sure the rent is paid on time. They are well worth the small percentage fee they charge."

Sarah nodded. The reasons made good sense to her.

"Remember, cheap does not mean good value," the Coach continued. "A cheap property manager, who is badly organized and causes you four weeks vacancy a year through the poor management of tenants and the bad administration of your property, will *cost you money!*"

"So, I guess that means another round of interviews, Coach. This will be fun," Brian liked the idea of building a solid team.

> **Leasing/Management Agent—**
> **It doesn't pay for me to go it alone here; for the price**
> **they charge, they are worth every cent. But I must know**
> **how to evaluate the good from the ordinary.**

"Let's look at appraisers next, shall we?" the Coach asked.

"Use a quality appraiser who is approved by your bank. Appraisers assess the current market value of a property by comparing the property you are looking at with other similar sales in the surrounding area. Many appraisers or real estate valuation Web sites offer quick estimation services for a minimal fee—they will give you an accurate guide to what the property is worth. If you think an appraiser has valued a property too low, challenge her on her appraisal with supporting house sales data and don't be afraid to get another appraisal as a second opinion if you need to."

Sarah looked up from her notes and asked, "What is the difference between the appraiser and the chattels valuer, Coach? I mean, can't we just use one valuer? Why do we need two?"

"Good question, Sarah. Chattel is "movable property"—an item of personal property that is not freehold land and is not intangible. See, like I've just explained, appraisers place a value on the property you have just bought or are thinking of buying. But the chattel valuer is an essential team member and one

I'm never without. I send one through every property I purchase. You see, they are experts at providing a comprehensive report on every possible item I can claim a paper tax deduction on. Their report lists every item, its value, and what percentage I can depreciate it at on my next tax return. They can also give an accurate estimation of the cost of renovations that were done in the past."

Brian was quick to add, "and Coach, we want all the deductions we can get, since that's the fourth income stream from our investment, isn't it?"

"Great thinking, Brian. You're getting focused; I like it." The Coach was really starting to see his students had come a long way.

Valuers/Chattel Valuers—
Obtaining an independent and accurate valuation is
crucial when it comes to using the equity I have in my
investment property, and the only way to get my tax
deductions is to have the chattels valued.

"Get to know a good builder—a tradesman, not a hammer hand," the Coach began, much to the amusement of Brian. Sarah had always teased him for his clumsiness when it came to tools.

"You want a professional job done. So many people try and save a dollar by getting a cheap, unqualified person who ruins the job and costs them more in the long run fixing up his mistakes. Real estate is a long-term asset; make sure you approach all renovations or repairs to your properties with a long-term view."

"But isn't it also about maximizing our dollar, Coach? I mean, if we can get the job done just as well by doing it ourselves, then surely we will be saving?" Brian added.

"Take time to first understand the rules that apply here, Brian," the Coach responded. "For instance, in many countries all contractors doing building work above a certain value are required to hold a tradesperson's certificate or contractor's licence. This could include, for example, painters, tilers, structural landscapers, carpenters, and builders. In most cases pest controllers, plumbers, and gas fitters are all required to have certification as part of their trade in any case. Always ask to see their credentials, check them out, and do your due diligence before you add them to your team."

Brian nodded. "That's interesting and good to know, Coach."

"Renovations or alterations that involve the coordination of several trades as part of the overall job, such as a plumber, tiler, plasterer, painter, and carpenter should only be conducted by a licensed builder," the Coach added. Sarah took notes relentlessly as she knew this was an area they would in all likelihood be pursuing.

"And remember, a trade contractor such as a licensed carpenter cannot conduct work that involves other trades."

This was news to Brian.

"And one other thing: If you want to do this work yourself, be aware that you need to check first with your local building authority to see what the rules are. In some states and countries, if the work you want to carry out yourself is over a set amount, you'll need to get an owner/builder's license or even be required to complete an owner/builder's course first."

Brian whistled in amazement.

"Be aware, too, that it's not always cheaper doing it yourself. The builder will have established relationships with other tradespeople like painters, electricians, plumbers, and plasterers who will be part of his team. They will generally charge a conservative rate because of the relationship they have with the builder. However, if you were to contract a plasterer directly, for instance, you probably wouldn't know if you were paying above the going rate or being overcharged."

Contractors—
Renovations, gardens, and cosmetic changes mean I need
to have several contractors in each area. Remember,
reliability is worth more than a cheap price in most cases.

"So, who else will be on your team and vital to your investing success?" The Coach kept the fast pace of the session going.

"Coach, we haven't discussed bankers yet," Sarah noticed.

"OK, great. Obviously we have a huge choice when it comes to borrowing money. There are bankers, brokers, and every other type of lender, but I prefer to deal with the bigger financial institutions myself."

"Why's that, Coach?" was Brian's only thought.

"It's simple: As I grow they have the ability to come with me. I work with on average five bankers and maybe one or two brokers at any one point in time and try to spread my borrowings around. Why do you think I spread my borrowings around?" The Coach was keeping them on their toes.

Sarah spotted the obvious reason. "So no one can have power over you, they each only have a percentage of your loans."

"Excellent answer, Sarah. Now when you get into the game you'll become well aware of current interest rates, packages, and trends, and you can often ask each banker to better the other's offer, but let's get back to getting your team together." The Coach changed tack a little.

Brian jumped in. "Coach, if we put together about three lenders up front, that should be plenty for us as beginners wouldn't you think?"

"Brian, you're on the money again."

Financiers—
Without access to the best financing available, my best investment intentions will come to nothing. I need a team of bankers whom I can choose from for each and every deal.

"So, group, the last person you'll need on your team up front for when you want to rent a property are all the retailers who will supply the house fittings and so on," the Coach began.

"Just because you wouldn't necessarily live in the investment property you have just bought doesn't mean it should be badly presented. You really do have a moral and even a financial obligation to ensure it is liveable and as pleasant as possible for your tenants. See, they will be the ones paying off the majority of your investment for you, so do the right thing and make their new home appealing."

Sarah nodded; this was her territory.

"But apart from that, it will give you an edge in the rental marketplace," the Coach added.

"What sorts of things are you thinking about, Coach?" Brian hated shopping.

Sarah jumped in. "You must be talking about light fixtures, carpets, bathroom fixtures, and all the things you would clean up when you add value through renovation."

The Coach passed out his notes again.

Retailers—
I can make any rental property look very appealing and livable by calling on an expert team of retailers to add the finishing touches to my new rental property.

"So how do you suggest we operate with a good real estate agent, Coach?" Sarah asked. "Once we have found one, that is."

"To begin with, and especially when I am entering a new area, I phone three or four real estate offices to make appointments with the top agent in each office," the Coach explained.

"Why do you want the top agent?" Brian interjected.

"Who has negotiated more deals than anyone else in the office?" the Coach asked.

"Who knows the area best of all? Who is intimately in touch with the market? Who has the widest base of local contacts? Who is the best negotiator? The office's top agent, of course!"

Brian felt mildly embarrassed but didn't regret the question. He had long since learned that the only silly question is the one that nobody asks.

"In the interview process, if I come across one that impresses me, remember that I offer to pay for a few hours of her time if she'll show me around the marketplace," the Coach continued.

"These top agents are always more than happy to do this without being paid. You see, they will gladly show me around because they know I could be the source of their next commission check. In fact, if they do a good job I could be the source of their next several commission checks! But I make the offer to pay for their time nevertheless because it shows them I'm a serious buyer who isn't wasting their time."

Brian nodded.

"When the agent shows me a hot deal and the numbers look good, we enter into negotiations. If at all possible I negotiate directly with the seller rather than through the agent simply because I don't trust the average agent to do this as well as I can. Good agents are worth their weight in gold, but they are harder to find than hen's teeth!"

The Coach paused to let that sink in. Then he continued.

"Now I never begrudge the agents their commissions. I'm always more than willing to pay them what they're due; it's just that I don't want them doing my dealing for me if I can avoid it."

"So how do you get around that, Coach?" Brian had forgotten the Coach's strategy, but like any good Coach he was happy to go over it again to make sure it was understood, so Sarah listened through it again, hoping to get a few new ideas.

"Simple. After they've shown me the property for the first time, I return later that evening, knock on the door, and say, 'I was here earlier today with your agent, and I just love the place. In fact it's the best I've seen so far. We were just driving past on our way home, and my wife asked me what color the bathroom is. I just couldn't remember, so I thought I'd stop by. Mind if I have another look?' They rarely ever refuse. And then I say, 'I'm ready to make an offer, but rather than waste time going to see the agent, I'd like to talk directly with you here and now. Of course, I'm more than willing to pay the agent a commission because she is the one who led me to you,' I always add. Then we verbally negotiate and we head to the agent together to draw up the contract and get it signed."

Brian smiled. Man, he is good, he thought to himself, and I do remember he told me that once before.

"I prefer making the offer direct. What seller would run the risk of losing a sale just because the agent wasn't the one conveying the offer? And in cases where I see a 'For Sale' sign up outside a property, I've been known to go straight up, knock on the door, view the property, negotiate the deal, then drive around to the agent and hand over a check for his commission. You should see the surprised look on his face! In cases like that, I make an ally for life. That agent becomes part of my team and understands how I like to operate."

"In many cases, however, you will have to work through Realtors, so you need to build rapport and get them working for you so they help you buy at a great price. Ever had an agent who was selling a property for you say something like the following? 'Well, the market is showing us we were wrong when we estimated the price.' " The Coach saw Brian nodding.

"That means the agent is working for the buyer trying to get the seller down in price. Always remember a good agent wants to make a deal and will sway the buyer or the seller to change the offer, usually the one the agent sees as being easiest to sway." The Coach had kept them really thinking this entire session.

One more handout and they were almost done.

Working with Real Estate Agents—
My agents or brokers are trying to run a business
and I need to keep that in mind as I work with
them. Doing this well will help me to achieve the best
possible results, not only when I buy properties but
also when the time comes for me to sell.

"The final topic we need to discuss today relates to the practicalities of owning an investment property. You see, sooner or later you will probably end up dealing with a property manager."

"I was wondering when this would come up," said Sarah. "I have a friend who works in real estate and it's an area that has always interested me."

"Once you have your investment property," the Coach began, "it needs to be properly managed. Good management techniques will maximize your investment return, and this is important because it's the reason you invested in real estate in the first place."

Sarah nodded.

"When it comes to managing our investment property, Coach, do we have any choices?" she asked.

"You bet. You basically have two choices. You can manage it yourself, or you can appoint a professional property manager to do this for you."

Sarah chuckled to herself, slightly embarrassed. That, she thought, should have been obvious.

"Presuming we decide to hire a property manager, how do we find a good one?" she asked. "We've all heard horror stories about incompetent property managers who don't care about your property or whether it's vacant for months on end. So what do we do to ensure we don't end up locked into a term contract with a poorly performing property manager?"

"Great question, Sarah," the Coach replied, but before he could go on, Brian jumped in and said, "How would we even recognize a good property manager from a bad one?"

The Coach waited for a moment and then said, "Interview your prospective property manager first; remember he works for you so treat the appointment with due care and consideration. Here's what I would do. Write this down.

1. Ask for references of other investors who have real estate in the same area as your property, and phone at least three of them.

2. Ask about the area to test his knowledge.

3. Make sure he credit checks all tenants before he rents the property to them. I have saved thousands of dollars in lost rent just by using a property manager who does credit checks when my old property manager didn't.

4. Ask how often he conducts inspections on the property and what form his reports take.

5. Ask to see a copy of the monthly and quarterly management report that would be sent to you. What you'll be looking for here is meaningful documentation. Many agents just produce sheets of paper with boxes ticked. These are not good enough. A detailed report to the owner is what I expect.

6. Get him to give you a written rental appraisal of your property and what he believes it should rent for. Check to see if this is accurate with several other real estate agents who work in the area.

7. Ask how he handles repairs to your property. I have a standing order with my property manager that if something needs fixing and it's under $250 he takes care of it and doesn't even bother me. I have to approve any expenditure over $251.

8. Check if he pays your rent to you weekly, biweekly, or monthly. Payment weekly or biweekly is a big bonus because this enables you to minimize any interest you may have on a line of credit account, and it's much better for cashflow!

9. Ask how long he has been established and what his experience is.

10. Ask to see the tenancy agreements he uses and read it carefully.

11. And, of course, check his fees. In my experience 7–8 percent of the rental income is reasonable. Usually the cheapest property managers are not good value for your money.

"Make sure the property manager's contract can be terminated by you in between 48 hours and 7 days should he fail to fulfil the terms of the contract.

"Speak to the agent about the techniques he uses to ensure vacancy periods are minimized. Ask about the timing of the commencement and expiry of fixed-term lease or rental agreements. Will he open your property for inspection on

Sundays? This is preferable, as many tenants would prefer to select a property on the weekend and sign the lease then and there rather than having to take a day off during the week for this."

Sarah thought for a moment and then asked if the Coach could give them an insight into the working relationship he has with his own property manager.

"My property manager is excellent!" the Coach responded. "When I buy a property, I advise him, then he goes down to the property and views it and then calls me. He advises me that if I replace the carpet, paint the hall, and repair the cracked window (he confirms quoted prices for doing all of this) at a cost of $1276, he can get a weekly rental of $250 instead of $200.

"Now you don't have to be a rocket scientist to work out that by spending $1276 I get back $2600 in the first year. That's a 100+ percent return on my investment."

Sarah was impressed.

"His value to me is his expertise and the *time* he saves me because all I have to do is say, 'Yes, make it happen,' and he coordinates and manages the entire process. Not only that but because I let him know about my purchase four weeks before I settle on it, he has four weeks to find great tenants and arranges for them to move in on settlement day, so I have rent rolling in from day one."

"That's fantastic, Coach," Sarah said. "I bet there can't be too many managers around like him."

"Once I had a truck back into one of my rental properties and take the corner off it," the Coach smiled. "My property manager called me while I was in line up at Subway buying lunch. He said, 'Just calling to let you know a truck has backed into your house on Wilson Street. We have a builder on the way and have organized the claim with the insurance company and the insurance assessor. You don't have to do anything, but I thought you might like to know in case you drove past and saw the damage.'

"You know, lunch was all the more enjoyable, knowing I had a great player on my team who made playing the game a whole lot easier."

The Coach leaned back in his chair, rubbed his hands through his hair, and stretched. It had been a long day. And a very successful and rewarding one.

**Choosing a Property Manager or Going It Alone—
While going it alone seems cheaper, in the long
run you will most probably decide you should
have used a property manager.**

Part 11

▌Four Green Houses
Become One Red Hotel

It was with mixed emotions that Brian and Sarah arrived at the Coach's office for their final structured coaching session. On the one hand, they were looking forward to getting on with what they had been learning, and on the other, they knew they would miss the weekly discipline, the interaction, and the stimulation that the Coach had given them.

They were now on the final stretch and could see the finish line. They also knew that this was not to be the end of their association with their Coach.

As they made their way to the now familiar door, Brian put his arm around his wife and said, "You know, this has been the start of one heck of a journey."

"Yes," Sarah responded, "and I agree. I have a real feeling it's only just started."

The Coach opened the door on the second knock and beckoned them in.

"How are you two?" he asked as he stood aside. "Are you ready for what lies ahead?"

"We're feeling both excited and nervous," Sarah replied. "It's a strange feeling, Coach. But I expect it's the same with everyone at this stage of the game."

The Coach smiled. He had seen this all too often before.

"There's one final thing we need to talk about still," the Coach began, "and that gets to the very heart of investing in real estate. See, you now know the basics, the mechanics, of how to go about buying an investment property for the best possible price, how to fund it, and how to manage it. But you need to remember what you are doing this for."

Brian nodded.

"You will most probably begin by buying modest properties just to get the ball rolling and some cashflow coming in. And you'll be learning as you go. As you build your wealth wheels, the time will come when you will be ready to begin looking at bigger and better properties, ones that will return you more money each month."

Sarah nodded in agreement.

"You will reach the point where you will decide the time is right to follow this path. So how will you do that?"

"By trading up," Brian replied.

"Exactly. And you may very well have to sell four modest properties to buy one bigger one, just like in Monopoly."

Trading Up—
As in Monopoly, four green houses eventually
become one red hotel. Eventually I will trade up
from some of the smaller deals I have done into
bigger and better-returning properties.

"One of the tricks in this game is to profit several times when the market moves," the Coach continued. "It's those who have bought well—remember what I said about profit being based on the purchase price and not the selling?—who will benefit most when the market moves upwards."

Sarah was writing as Brian absorbed what was being said.

"You'll notice a market move and of course the inner city will go first, so ride the wave as it moves from bigger cities to smaller ones and from the city center out. If you time it right you can ride a growth cycle two or even three times and get huge gains in a short period of time."

The Coach was ready to keep going when Brian spoke up. "So, Coach, do we sell the inner city ones or just redraw and move out to find the suburbs that haven't boomed yet?"

"You can do either, but as you know I prefer to never sell, just to redraw. At times like these, you can also do the quick cash deals because there will inevitably be a buying frenzy taking place. This is the time to stick to your plan, jump in and buy, renovate, and resell, or buy and revalue so that you can make use of the additional equity your properties now have. And remember, you should be aiming to do this at least twice during each growth cycle."

> **Riding the Growth Cycles—**
> **Every 10 years or so the market has a 2- to**
> **3-year growth spurt. I want to buy and revalue**
> **at least twice during this boom cycle.**

"You also need to prepare for the slower cycles that are sure to follow boom cycles as sure as night follows day," the Coach continued.

"What do you mean by that, Coach?" Brian asked.

"You need to make sure your plan includes sitting tight at times; in other words, you must not bank on buying and selling continually to arrive at your ultimate goal. There will be times when it just doesn't pay to sell because the figures won't add up. You could, for instance, be looking at hardly recovering your costs if you were to sell. And considering the aim of the game is to make money, not lose it, you would be better off holding onto your properties and earning the rental income they produce."

"Ah, I see," Sarah commented. "And we would use this time to prepare for the next boom cycle by doing our market research."

The Coach nodded. He could see his students had learned a lot since they first came to him.

"You have to allow a little room for the increases in interest rates that will undoubtedly come along and essentially remember the simple rule of property, that if you can afford to hold you will always make money in the long run." The Coach gave them one of the last few notes they would ever need from him.

> **Holding through Slow and Down Times—**
> After every boom comes a down cycle and
> then slower times. I need to make sure my
> portfolio will be easy to hold during this time
> and get ready for the next boom cycle.

"The one thing you must continually be mindful of is adding to or increasing the value of your properties, because this is the surest way you can make more rent. It will also ensure you earn more when you finally sell."

Sarah understood exactly what the Coach was saying.

"So when we are able to attract a higher rent for our properties, then we will have a better chance of having them valued higher by an appraiser, right, Coach?"

"That's the idea, Sarah. It acts like a circle; the more you can increase the value of a property, the more you can rent it for. And the more you rent it for, the higher its value becomes."

"And I guess the best way to get the ball rolling is to renovate?" Brian added, not wanting to be left out of the discussion.

"That's right. That is why I regard renovations as an investment."

> **Renovation Speeds It Up—**
> Renovation adds value at any time in the cycle;
> as you renovate you raise rents, and as rents go up
> so does value. It's just a matter of adding more
> value than it costs to renovate.

They had covered a whole lot more than they had expected. Brian was more than delighted and Sarah felt that she was a lot smarter than she had often believed.

This session had done wonders for her self-esteem and for that she was more than grateful.

But they were not yet through. The Coach showed no signs of finishing.

"So far we have been concentrating on residential property," he began. "There are, as you will now appreciate, very many compelling reasons for doing so from an investment point of view, especially as a beginner. But there are nevertheless other forms of property in which we can invest. You need to understand them, particularly as far as they compare to residential real estate."

Brian nodded. "I was wondering whether we would cover that at all," he remarked.

"I'm often asked about the pros and cons of investing in other forms of property," the Coach went on.

"Now I know many people have made good money from commercial property, but as a general rule, when you start, it is less risky if you to stick with residential property. Let me explain why. Commercial, industrial, retail, and hospitality property possess all the attributes of a good investment but involve risks beyond your control. Business managers generally become your tenants and if they do a poor job managing their businesses, they may not be able to pay the rent.

"Also, business downturns, changing consumer trends, the fact that businesses usually take months to move into new premises, and all sorts of other factors could mean you don't get paid or go without a tenant for months or even years at a time. If you own a building that has six shops, three of which are empty for even just a few months, what sort of interest do you think that would generate from prospective buyers, should you decide to sell? Not to mention the impact it will have on your cashflow."

"Very good points, Coach," Brian said.

"But the time may come when we are confident enough, when we know enough, and when our resources are large enough to allow us to diversify and consider owning some commercial property," Sarah said.

"That's my point, Sarah. Commercial property does have many attractions for the investor, but as I've said, better to cut your teeth as property investors in the residential market. But we'll talk more about that when the time comes. In the meantime, go now and begin building your real estate investment portfolio. Go and start building your first Property Wealth Wheel."

**Time to Consider Commercial Property?—
Once my residential portfolio has reached stability,
it may be time to think about growing into the next level
of property investing—commercial property.**

Part 12

▪ Catching Up

It had been just about four years since the Coach had seen his students.

For at least two years after their meetings finished they would speak to the Coach at least once every month, more often every week, to show him their deals and make sure they were meeting their rules, but as the Coach took on new students he had to let Brian and Sarah go their own way.

"Wow, Coach, you haven't changed a bit," Sarah said as she gave him a big hug of welcome.

"And wow, you look great, and that new outfit looks great on you. I think you must be doing well." The Coach was remembering how far the couple had come.

They were having dinner together at not only the best restaurant in town, but at the best table, and Brian had already chosen the wine from the cellar.

"Hi, Brian. Great to see you as well." The Coach was excited to talk real estate with them again.

They sat and dined and Sarah showed the Coach pictures of their now nine investment properties and the two deals they had bought, renovated, and sold.

Everyone was laughing and really enjoying life; it was really a night that showed exactly what dedication and discipline could do over time. They celebrated the couple's success with gusto, and you could see the pride in the Coach's eyes.

Brain had all the numbers to show the Coach so he could also get in on the party and prove that they had negotiated well, followed their rules, and really built a great team around them.

As the night came to a close Brian asked the waiter for a package he had asked him to hold earlier. It was a gift for the Coach.

"Coach, we wanted to get you something so you know just how much we think about you every day, and how much we use your lessons with every deal we do." Brian handed him the gift as he spoke.

The Coach was truly proud that they still understood gratitude now that they had built a solid level of wealth and cashflow, and as he opened his gift he thanked them both profusely. It was a frame with a family photo—Brian and Sarah with all their properties.

It was time to go when the Coach pulled one last note from his pocket, and it reminded both Brian and Sarah of why they were so appreciative of everything the Coach had given them.

Getting into *Action*—
Every great decision will either scare the life
out of you or excite the pants off you, so scare
or excite yourself more often.

Getting into *Action*

So, when is the best time to start?

Now—right now—so let me give you a step-by-step method to get yourself onto the same success path of many of my clients and the clients of my team at *Action International.*

Start testing and measuring now.

You'll want to ask your customers and prospects how they found out about you and your business. This will give you an idea of what's been working and what hasn't. You also want to concentrate on the five areas of the business chassis. Remember:

1. Number of Leads from each campaign.
2. Conversion Rate from each and every campaign.
3. Number of Transactions on average per year per customer.
4. Average Dollar Sale from each campaign.
5. Your Margins on each product or service.

The Number of Leads is easy; just take a measure for four weeks, average it out, and multiply by 50 working weeks of the year. Of course you'd ask each lead where they came from so you've got enough information to make advertising decisions.

The Conversion Rate is a little trickier, not because it's hard to measure, but because we want to know a few more details. You want to know what level of conversion you have from each and every type of marketing strategy you use. Remember that some customers won't buy right away, so keep accurate records on each and every lead.

To find the Number of Transactions you'll need to go through your records. Hopefully you can find the transaction history of at least 50 of your past customers and then average out their yearly purchases.

The Average Dollar Sale is as simple as it sounds. The total dollars sold divided by the number of sales. The best information you can collect is the average from each marketing campaign you run, so that you know where the real profit is coming from.

And, of course, your margins. An Average Margin is good to know and measure, but to know the margins on everything you sell is the most powerful knowledge you can collect.

If you're having any challenges with your testing and measuring, be sure to contact your nearest *Action International* Business Coach. She'll be able to help you through and show you the specialized documents to use.

If, by chance, you're thinking of racing ahead before you test and measure, remember this. It's impossible to improve a score when you don't know what the score is.

So you've got your starting point. You know exactly what's going on in your business right now. In fact, you know more about not only what's happening right now, but also the factors that are going to create what will happen tomorrow.

The next step in your business growth is simple.

Let's decide what you want out of the business—in other words, your goals. Here are the main points I want you to plan for.

How many hours do you want to work each week? How much money do you want to take out of the business each month? And, most importantly, when do you want to finish the business?

By "finish" the business, I mean when it will be systematized enough so it can run without your having to be there. Remember this about business; a little bit of planning goes a long way, but to make a plan you have to have a destination.

Once again, if you're having difficulty, talk to an *Action International* Business Coach. He'll know exactly how to help you find what it is you really want out of both your business and your life.

Now the real work begins.

Remember, our goal is to get a 10 percent increase in each area over the next 12 months. Choose well, but I want to warn you of one thing, one thing I can literally guarantee.

Eight out of 10 marketing campaigns you run *will not work.*

That's why when you choose to run, say, an advertising campaign in your local newspaper, you've got to run at least 10 different ads. When you select a direct mail campaign, you should send out at least 10 different letters to test, and so on.

Make sure you get at least five strategies under each heading and plan to run at least one, preferably two, at least each month for the next 12 months.

Don't work on just one of the five areas at a time; mix it up a little so you get the synergy of all five areas working together.

Now, this is the most important advice I can give you:

Learn how to make each and every strategy work. Don't just think you know what to do; go through my hints and tips, read more books, listen to as many tapes as you can, watch all the videos you can find, talk to the experts, and make sure you get the most advantage you can before you invest a whole lot of money.

The next 12 months are going to be a matter of doing the numbers, running the campaigns, testing headlines, testing offers, testing prices, and, of course, measuring the results.

By the end of it you should have at least five new strategies in each of the five areas working together to produce a great result.

Once again I want to stress that this will work and this will make your business grow as long as *you* work it.

Is it simple? *Yes.*

Is it easy? *No.*

You'll have to work hard. If you can get the guidance of someone who's been there before you, then get it.

Whatever you do, start it now, start it today, and most importantly, make the most of every day. Your past does not equal your future; you decide your future right here and right now.

Be who you want to be, *do* what you need to do, in order to *have* what you want to have.

Positive *thought* without positive *Action* leaves you with positively *nothing.* I called my company *Action International,* not Theory International, or Yeah, I read that book International, but *Action International.*

So take the first step—and get into *Action.*

■ ABOUT THE AUTHOR

Bradley J. Sugars

Brad Sugars is a world-renowned Australian entrepreneur, author, and business coach who has helped more than a million clients around the world find business and personal success.

He's a trained accountant, but as he puts it, most of his experience comes from owning his own companies. Brad's been in business for himself since age 15 in some way or another, although his father would argue he started at 7 when he was caught selling his Christmas presents to his brothers. He's owned and operated more than two dozen companies, from pizza to ladies fashion, from real estate to insurance and many more.

His main company, *Action International*, started from humble beginnings in the back bedroom of a suburban home in 1993 when Brad started teaching business owners how to grow their sales and marketing results. Now *Action* has nearly 1000 franchises in 19 countries and is ranked in the top 100 franchises in the world.

Brad Sugars has spoken on stage with the likes of Tom Hopkins, Brian Tracy, John Maxwell, Robert Kiyosaki, and Allen Pease, written books with people like Anthony Robbins, Jim Rohn, and Mark Victor Hansen, appeared on countless TV and radio programs and in literally hundreds of print articles around the globe. He's been voted as one of the Most Admired Entrepreneurs by the readers of *E-Spy* magazine—next to the likes of Rupert Murdoch, Henry Ford, Richard Branson, and Anita Roddick.

Today, *Action International* has coaches across the globe and is ranked as one of the Top 25 Fastest Growing Franchises on the planet as well as the #1 Business Consulting Franchise. The success of *Action International* is simply attributed to the fact that they apply the strategies their coaches use with business owners.

Brad is a proud father and husband, the chairman of a major childrens' charity and in his own words, "a very average golfer."

Check out Brad's Web site www.bradsugars.com and read the literally hundreds of testimonials from those who've gone before you.

■ RECOMMENDED READING LIST

ACTION INTERNATIONAL BOOK LIST

"The only difference between *you* now and *you* in 5 years' time will be the people you meet and the books you read." Charlie Tremendous Jones

"And, the only difference between *your* income now and *your* income in 5 years' time will be the people you meet, the books you read, the tapes you listen to, and then how *you* apply it all." Brad Sugars

- *The E-Myth Revisited* by Michael E. Gerber
- *My Life in Advertising & Scientific Advertising* by Claude Hopkins
- *Tested Advertising Methods* by John Caples
- *Building the Happiness Centered Business* by Dr. Paddi Lund
- *Write Language* by Paul Dunn & Alan Pease
- *7 Habits of Highly Effective People* by Steven Covey
- *First Things First* by Steven Covey
- *Awaken the Giant Within* by Anthony Robbins
- *Unlimited Power* by Anthony Robbins
- *22 Immutable Laws of Marketing* by Al Ries & Jack Trout
- *21 Ways to Build a Referral Based Business* by Brad Sugars
- *21 Ways to Increase Your Advertising Response* by Mark Tier
- *The One Minute Salesperson* by Spencer Johnson & Larry Wilson
- *The One Minute Manager* by Spencer Johnson & Kenneth Blanchard
- *The Great Sales Book* by Jack Collis
- *Way of the Peaceful Warrior* by Dan Millman
- *How to Build a Championship Team*—Six Audio tapes by Blair Singer
- Brad Sugars "Introduction to Sales & Marketing" 3-hour Video
- Leverage—Board Game by Brad Sugars
- *17 Ways to Increase Your Business Profits* booklet & tape by Brad Sugars. FREE OF CHARGE to Business Owners

*To order Brad Sugars' products from the recommended reading list, call your nearest *Action International* office today.

The 18 Most Asked Questions about Working with an *Action International* Business Coach

And 18 great reasons why you'll jump at the chance to get your business flying and make your dreams come true

1. So who is *Action International?*

Action International is a business Coaching and Consulting company started in 1993 by entrepreneur and author Brad Sugars. With offices around the globe and business coaches from Singapore to Sydney to San Francisco, *Action International* has been set up with you, the business owner, in mind.

Unlike traditional consulting firms, *Action* is designed to give you both short-term assistance and long-term training through its affordable Mentoring approach. After 12 years teaching business owners how to succeed, *Action's* more than 10,000 clients and 1,000,000 seminar attendees will attest to the power of the programs.

Based on the sales, marketing, and business management systems created by Brad Sugars, your *Action* Coach is trained to not only show you how to increase your business revenues and profits, but also how to develop the business so that you as the owner work less and relax more.

Action International is a franchised company, so your local *Action* Coach is a fellow business owner who's invested her own time, money, and energy to make her business succeed. At *Action,* your success truly does determine our success.

2. And, why do I need a Business Coach?

Every great sports star, business person, and superstar is surrounded by coaches and advisors.

And, as the world of business moves faster and gets more competitive, it's difficult to keep up with both the changes in your industry and the innovations in sales, marketing, and management strategies. Having a business coach is no longer a luxury; it's become a necessity.

On top of all that, it's impossible to get an objective answer from yourself. Don't get me wrong. You can survive in business without the help of a Coach, but it's almost impossible to thrive.

A Coach *can* see the forest for the trees. A Coach will make you focus on the game. A Coach will make you run more laps than you feel like. A Coach will tell it like it is. A Coach will give you small pointers. A Coach will listen. A Coach will be your marketing manager, your sales director, your training coordinator, your partner, your confidant, your mentor, your best friend, and an *Action* Business Coach will help you make your dreams come true.

3. Then, what's an Alignment Consultation?

Great question. It's where an *Action* Coach starts with every business owner. You'll invest a minimum of $1295, and during the initial 2 to 3 hours your Coach invests with you, he'll learn as much as he can about your business, your goals, your challenges, your sales, your marketing, your finances, and so much more.

All with three goals in mind: To know exactly where your business is now. To clarify your goals both in the business and personally. And thirdly, to get the crucial pieces of information he needs to create your businesses *Action* Plan for the next 12 months.

Not a traditional business or marketing plan mind you, but a step-by-step plan of *Action* that you'll work through as you continue with the Mentor Program.

4. So, what, then, is the Mentor Program?

Simply put, it's where your *Action* Coach will work with you for a full 12 months to make your goals a reality. From weekly coaching calls and goal-setting sessions, to creating marketing pieces together, you will develop new sales strategies and business systems so you can work less and learn all that you need to know about how to make your dreams come true.

You'll invest between $995 and $10,000 a month and your Coach will dedicate a minimum of 5 hours a month to working with you on your sales, marketing, team building, business development, and every step of the *Action* Plan you created from your Alignment Consultation.

Unlike most consultants, your *Action* Coach will do more than just show you what to do. She'll be with you when you need her most, as each idea takes shape, as each campaign is put into place, as you need the little pointers on making it happen, when you need someone to talk to, when you're faced with challenges and, most importantly, when you're just not sure what to do next. Your Coach will be there every step of the way.

5. Why at least 12 months?

If you've been in business for more than a few weeks, you've seen at least one or two so called "quick fixes."

Most Consultants seem to think they can solve all your problems in a few hours or a few days. At *Action* we believe that long-term success means not just scraping the surface and doing it for you. It means doing it with you, showing you how to do it, working alongside you, and creating the success together.

Over the 12 months, you'll work on different areas of your business, and month by month you'll not only see your goals become a reality, you'll gain both the confidence and the knowledge to make it happen again and again, even when your first 12 months of Coaching is over.

6. How can you be sure this will work in my industry and in my business?

Very simple. You see at *Action,* we're experts in the areas of sales, marketing, business development, business management, and team building just to name a few. With 328 different profit-building strategies, you'll soon see just how powerful these systems are.

You, on the other hand, are the expert in your business and together we can apply the *Action* systems to make your business fly.

Add to this the fact that within the *Action* Team at least one of our Coaches has either worked with, managed, worked in, or even owned a business that's the same or very similar to yours. Your *Action* Coach has the full resources of the entire *Action* team to call upon for every challenge you have. Imagine hundreds of experts ready to help you.

7. Won't this just mean more work?

Of course when you set the plan with your *Action* Coach, it'll all seem like a massive amount of work, but no one ever said attaining your goals would be easy.

In the first few months, it'll take some work to adjust, some work to get over the hump so to speak. The further you are into the program, the less and less work you'll have to do.

You will, however, be literally amazed at how focused you'll be and how much you'll get done. With focus, an *Action* Coach, and most importantly the *Action* Systems, you'll be achieving a whole lot more with the same or even less work.

8. How will I find the time?

Once again the first few months will be the toughest, not because of an extra amount of work, but because of the different work. In fact, your *Action* Coach will show you how to, on a day-to-day basis, get more work done with less effort.

In other words, after the first few months you'll find that you're not working more, just working differently. Then, depending on your goals from about month six onwards, you'll start to see the results of all your work, and if you choose to, you can start working less than ever before. Just remember, it's about changing what you do with your time, *not* putting in more time.

9. How much will I need to invest?

Nothing, if you look at it from the same perspective as we do. That's the difference between a cost and an investment. Everything you do with your *Action* Coach is a true investment in your future.

Not only will you create great results in your business, but you'll end up with both an entrepreneurial education second to none, and the knowledge that you can repeat your successes over and over again.

As mentioned, you'll need to invest at least $1295 up to $5000 for the Alignment Consultation and Training Day, and then between $995 and $10,000 a month for the next 12 months of coaching.

Your Coach may also suggest several books, tapes, and videos to assist in your training, and yes, they'll add to your investment as you go. Why? Because having an *Action* Coach is just like having a marketing manager, a sales team leader, a trainer, a recruitment specialist, and corporate consultant all for half the price of a secretary.

10. Will it cost me extra to implement the strategies?

Once again, give your *Action* Coach just half an hour and he'll show you how to turn your marketing into an investment that yields sales and profits rather than just running up your expenses.

In most cases we'll actually save you money when we find the areas that aren't working for you. But yes, I'm sure you'll need to spend some money to make some money.

Yet, when you follow our simple testing and measuring systems, you'll never risk more than a few dollars on each campaign, and when we find the ones that work, we make sure you keep profiting from them time and again.

Remember, when you go the accounting way of saving costs, you can only ever add a few percent to the bottom line.

Following Brad Sugars' formula, your *Action* Coach will show you that through sales, marketing, and income growth, your possible returns are exponential.

The sky's the limit, as they say.

11. Are there any guarantees?

To put it bluntly, no. Your *Action* Coach will never promise any specific results, nor will she guarantee that any of your goals will become a reality.

You see, we're your coach. You're still the player, and it's up to you to take the field. Your Coach will push you, cajole you, help you, be there for you, and even do some things with you, but you've still got to do the work.

Only *you* can ever be truly accountable for your own success and at *Action* we know this to be a fact. We guarantee to give you the best service we can, to answer your questions promptly, and with the best available information. And, last but not least your *Action* Coach is committed to making you successful whether you like it or not.

That's right, once we've set the goals and made the plan, we'll do whatever it takes to make sure you reach for that goal and strive with all your might to achieve all that you desire.

Of course we'll be sure to keep you as balanced in your life as we can. We'll make sure you never compromise either the long-term health and success of your company or yourself, and more importantly your personal set of values and what's important to you.

12. What results have other business owners seen?

Anything from previously working 60 hours a week down to working just 10—right through to increases in revenues of 100s and even 1000s of percent. Results speak for themselves. Be sure to keep reading for specific examples of real people, with real businesses, getting real results.

There are three reasons why this will work for you in your business. Firstly, your *Action* Coach will help you get 100 percent focused on your goals and the step-by-step processes to get you there. This focus alone is amazing in its effect on you and your business results.

Secondly, your coach will hold you accountable to get things done, not just for the day-to-day running of the business, but for the dynamic growth of the business. You're investing in your success and we're going to get you there.

Thirdly, your Coach is going to teach you one-on-one as many of *Action's* 328 profit-building strategies as you need. So whether your goal is to be making more money, or working fewer hours or both inside the next 12 months your goals can become a reality. Just ask any of the thousands of existing *Action* clients, or more specifically, check out the results of 19 of our most recent clients shown later in this section.

13. What areas will you coach me in?

There are five main areas your *Action* Coach will work on with you. Of course, how much of each depends on you, your business, and your goals.

Sales. The backbone of creating a superprofitable business, and one area we'll help you get spectacular results in.

Marketing and Advertising. If you want to get a sale, you've got to get a prospect. Over the next 12 months your *Action* Coach will teach you Brad Sugars' amazingly simple streetwise marketing—marketing that makes profits.

Team Building and Recruitment. You'll never *wish* for the right people again. You'll have motivated and passionate team members when your Coach shows you how.

Systems and Business Development. Stop the business from running you and start running your business. Your Coach will show you the secrets to having the business work, even when you're not there.

Customer Service. How to deliver consistently, make it easy to buy, and leave your customers feeling delighted with your service. Both referrals and repeat business are centered in the strategies your Coach will teach you.

14. Can you also train my people?

Yes. We believe that training your people is almost as important as coaching you.

Your investment starts at $1500 for your entire team, and you can decide between five very powerful in-house training programs. From *"Sales Made Simple"* for your face-to-face sales team to *"Phone Power"* for your entire team's telephone etiquette and sales ability. Then you can run the "*Raving Fans*" customer service training or the "*Total Team*" training. And finally, if you're too busy earning a living to make any real money, then you've just got to attend our "*Business Academy 101.*" It will make a huge impact on your finances, business, career, family, and lifestyle. You'll be amazed at how much involvement and excitement comes out of your team with each training program.

15. Can you write ads, letters, and marketing pieces for me?

Yes. Your *Action* Coach can do it for you, he can train you to do it yourself, or we can simply critique the marketing pieces you're using right now.

If you want us to do it for you, our one-time fees start at just $1195. You'll not only get one piece; we'll design several pieces for you to take to the market and see which one performs the best. Then, if it's a critique you're after, just $349 means we'll work through your entire piece and give you feedback on what to change, how to change it, and what else you should do. Last but not least, for between $15 and $795 we can recommend a variety of books, tapes, and most importantly, Brad Sugars' Instant Success series books that'll take you step-by-step through the how-tos of creating your marketing pieces.

16. Why do you also recommend books, tapes, and videos?

Basically, to save you time and money. Take Brad Sugars' *Sales Rich* DVD or Video Series, for instance. In about 16 hours you'll learn more about business than you have in the last 12 years. It'll also mean your *Action* Coach works with you on the high-level implementation rather than the very basic teaching.

It's a very powerful way for you to speed up the coaching process and get phenomenal rather than just great results.

17. When is the best time to get started?

Yesterday. OK, seriously, right now, today, this minute, before you take another step, waste another dollar, lose another sale, work too many more hours, miss another family event, forget another special occasion.

Far too many business people wait and see. They think working harder will make it all better. Remember, what you know got you to where you are. To get to where you want to go, you've got to make some changes and most probably learn something new.

There's no time like the present to get started on your dreams and goals.

18. So how do we get started?

Well, you'd better get back in touch with your *Action* Coach. There's some very simple paperwork to sign, and then you're on your way.

You'll have to invest a few hours showing them everything about your business. Together you'll get a plan created and then the work starts. Remember, it may seem like a big job at the start, but with a Coach, you're sharing the load and together you'll achieve great things.

Here's what others say about what happened after working with an *Action* business coach

Paul and Rosemary Rose—Icontact Multimedia

"Our *Action* coach showed us several ways to help market our product. We went on to triple our client base and simultaneously tripled our profits in just seven months. It was unbelievable! Last year was our best Christmas ever. We were really able to spoil ourselves!"

S. Ford—Pride Kitchens

"In 6 months, I've gone from working more than 60 hours per week in my business to less than 20, and my conversion rate's up from 19 percent to 62 percent. I've now got some life back!"

Gary and Leanne Paper—Galea Timber Products

"We achieved our goal for the 12 months within a 6-month period with a 100 percent increase in turnover and a good increase in margins. We have already recommended and will continue to recommend this program to others."

Russell, Kevin, John, and Karen—Northern Lights Power and Distribution

"Our profit margin has increased from 8 percent to 21 percent in the last 8 months. *Action* coaching focussed us on what are our most profitable markets."

Ty Pedersen—De Vries Marketing Sydney

"After just three months of coaching, my sales team's conversion rate has grown from an average of less than 12 percent to more than 23 percent and our profits have climbed by more than 30 percent."

Hank Meerkerk and Hemi McGarvey—B.O.P. School of Welding

"Last year we started off with a profit forecast, but as soon as we got *Action* involved we decided to double our forecast. We're already well over that forecast again by two-and-a-half times on turnover, and profits are even higher. Now we run a really profitable business."

Stuart Birch—Education Personnel Limited

"One direct mail letter added $40,000 to my bottom line, and working with *Action* has given me quality time to work on my business and spend time with my family."

Mark West—Wests Pumping and Irrigation

"In four months two simple strategies have increased our business more than 20 percent. We're so busy, we've had to delay expanding the business while we catch up!"

Michael Griffiths—Gym Owner

"I went from working 70 hours per week *in* the business to just 25 hours, with the rest of the time spent working *on* the business."

Cheryl Standring—In Harmony Landscapes

"We tried our own direct mail and only got a 1 percent response. With *Action* our response rate increased to 20 percent. It's definitely worth every dollar we've invested."

Jason and Chris Houston—Empradoor Finishing

"After 11 months of working with *Action,* we have increased our sales by 497 percent, and the team is working without our having to be there."

Michael Avery—Coomera Pet Motels

"I was skeptical at first, but I knew we needed major changes in our business. In 2 months, our extra profits were easily covering our investment and our predictions for the next 10 months are amazing."

Garry Norris—North Tax & Accounting

"As an accountant, my training enables me to help other business people make more money. It is therefore refreshing when someone else can help me do the same. I have a policy of only referring my clients to people who are professional, good at what they do, and who have personally given me great service. *Action* fits all three of these criteria, and I recommend *Action* to my business clients who want to grow and develop their businesses further."

Lisa Davis and Steve Groves—Mt. Eden Motorcycles

"With *Action* we increased our database from 800 to 1200 in 3 months. We consistently get about 20 new qualified people on our database each week for less than $10 per week."

Christine Pryor—U-Name-It Embroidery

"Sales for August this year have increased 352 percent. We're now targeting a different market and we're a lot more confident about what we're doing."

Joseph Saitta and Michelle Fisher—Banyule Electrics

"Working with *Action,* our inquiry rate has doubled. In four months our business has changed so much our customers love us. It's a better place for people to work and our margins are widening."

Kevin and Alison Snook—Property Sales

"In the 12 months previous to working with *Action,* we had sold one home in our subdivision. In the first eight months of working with *Action,* we sold six homes. The results speak for themselves."

Wayne Manson—Hospital Supplies

"When I first looked at the Mentoring Program it looked expensive, but from the inside looking out, its been the best money I have ever spent. Sales are up more than $3000 per month since I started, and the things I have learned and expect to learn will ensure that I will enjoy strong sustainable growth in the future."

■ *Action* Contact Details

Action International Asia Pacific

Ground Floor, *Action* House, 2 Mayneview Street, Milton QLD 4064

Ph: +61 (0) 7 3368 2525

Fax: +61 (0) 7 3368 2535

Free Call: 1800 670 335

Action International Europe

Olympic House, Harbor Road, Howth, Co. Dublin, Ireland

Ph: +353 (0) 1-8320213

Fax: +353 (0) 1-8394934

Action International North America

5670 Wynn Road Suite A & C, Las Vegas, Nevada 89118

Ph: +1 (702) 795 3188

Fax: +1 (702) 795 3183

Free Call: (888) 483 2828

Action International UK

3-5 Richmond Hill, Richmond, Surrey, TW 106RE

Ph: +44 020 8948 5151

Fax: +44 020 8948 4111

Action Offices around the globe:

Australia | Canada | China | England | France | Germany | Hong Kong

India | Indonesia | Ireland | Malaysia | Mexico | New Zealand

Phillippines | Scotland | Spain | Singapore | USA | Wales

Here's how you can profit from all of Brad's ideas with your local *Action* International **Business Coach**

Just like a sporting coach pushes an athlete to achieve optimum performance, provides them with support when they are exhausted, and teaches the athlete to execute plays that the competition does not anticipate.

A business coach will make you run more laps than you feel like. A business coach will show it like it is. And a business coach will listen.

The role of an *Action* Business Coach is to show you how to improve your business through guidance, support, and encouragement. Your coach will help you with your sales, marketing, management, team building, and so much more. Just like a sporting coach, your *Action* Business Coach will help you and your business perform at levels you never thought possible.

Whether you've been in business for a week or 20 years, it's the right time to meet with and see how you'll profit from an *Action* Coach.

As the owner of a business it's hard enough to keep pace with all the changes and innovations going on in your industry, let alone to find the time to devote to sales, marketing, systems, planning and team management, and then to run your business as well.

As the world of business moves faster and becomes more competitive, having a Business Coach is no longer a luxury; it has become a necessity. Based on the sales, marketing, and business management systems created by Brad Sugars, your *Action* Coach is trained to not only show you how to increase your business revenues and profits but also how to develop your business so that you, as the owner, can take back control. All with the aim of your working less and relaxing more. Making money is one thing; having the time to enjoy it is another.

Your *Action* Business Coach will become your marketing manager, your sales director, your training coordinator, your confidant, your mentor. In short, your *Action* Coach will help you make your business dreams come true.

ATTENTION BUSINESS OWNERS
You can increase your profits now

Here's how you can have one of Brad's *Action* International Business Coaches guide you to success.

Like every successful sporting icon or team, a business needs a coach to help it achieve its full potential. In order to guarantee your business success, you can have one of Brad's team as your business coach. You will learn about how you can get amazing results with the help of the team at *Action* International.

The business coaches are ready to take you and your business on a journey that will reward you for the rest of your life. You see, we believe *Action* speaks louder than words.

Complete and post this card to your local *Action* office to discover how our team can help you increase your income today!

Action International

The World's Number-1 Business Coaching Team

Name ....

Position ....

Company ....

Address ....

....

Country ....

Phone ....

Fax ....

Email ....

Referred by ....

How do I become an *Action* *International* **Business Coach?**

If you choose to invest your time and money in a great business and you're looking for a white-collar franchise opportunity to build yourself a lifestyle, an income, a way to take control of your life and, a way to get great personal satisfaction …

Then you've just found the world's best team!

Now, it's about finding out if you've got what it takes to really enjoy and thrive in this amazing business opportunity.

Here are the 4 things we look for in every *Action* Coach:

1. You've got to love succeeding

We're looking for people who love success, who love getting out there and making things happen. People who enjoy mixing with other people, people who thrive on learning and growing, and people who want to charge an hourly rate most professionals only dream of.

2. You've got to love being in charge of your own life

When you're ready to take control, the key is to be in business for yourself, but not by yourself. *Action*'s support, our training, our world leading systems, and the backup of a global team are all waiting to give you the best chance of being an amazing business success.

3. You've got to love helping people

Being a great Coach is all about helping yourself by helping others. The first time clients thank you for showing them step by step how to make more money and work less within their business, will be the day you realize just how great being an *Action* Business Coach really is.

4. You've got to love a great lifestyle

Working from home, setting your own timetable, spending time with family and friends, knowing that the hard work you do is for your own company and, not having to climb a so-called corporate ladder. This is what lifestyle is all about. Remember, business is supposed to give you a life, not take it away.

Our business is booming and we're seriously looking for people ready to find out more about how becoming a member of the *Action* *International* Business Coaching team is going to be the best decision you've ever made.

Apply online now at www.action-international.com

Here's how you can network, get new leads, build yourself an instant sales team, learn, grow and build a great team of supportive business owners around you by checking into your local *Action* Profit Club

Joining your local *Action* Profit Club is about more than just networking, it's also the learning and exchanging of profitable ideas.

Embark on a journey to a more profitable enterprise by meeting with fellow, like-minded business owners.

An ***Action*** Profit Club is an excellent way to network with business people and business owners. You will meet every two weeks for breakfast to network and learn profitable strategies to grow your business.

Here are three reasons why ***Action*** *International's* Profit Clubs work where other networking groups don't:

1. You know networking is a great idea. The challenge is finding the time and maintaining the motivation to keep it up and make it a part of your business. If you're not really having fun and getting the benefits, you'll find it gets easier to find excuses that stop you going. So, we guarantee you will always have fun and learn a lot from your bi-weekly group meetings.
2. The real problem is that so few people do any work 'on' their business. Instead they generally work "in" it, until it's too late. By being a member of an ***Action*** Profit Club, you get to attend FREE business-building workshops run by Business Coaches that teach you how to work "on" your business and avoid this common pitfall and help you to grow your business.
3. Unlike other groups, we have marketing systems to assist in your groups' growth rather than just relying on you to bring in new members. This way you can concentrate on YOUR business rather than on ours.

Latest statistics show that the average person knows at least 200 other contacts. By being a member of your local ***Action*** Profit Club, you have an instant network of around 3,000 people

Join your local *Action* Profit Club today.

Apply online now at www.actionprofitclub.com

LEVERAGE—The Game of Business
Your Business Success is just a Few Games Away

Leverage—The Game of Business is a fun way to learn how to succeed in business fast.

The rewards start flowing the moment you start playing!

Leverage is three hours of fun, learning, and discovering how you can be an amazingly successful business person.

It's a breakthrough in education that will have you racking up the profits in no time. The principles you take away from playing this game will set you up for a life of business success. It will open your mind to what's truly possible. Apply what you learn and **sit back and watch your profits soar.**

By playing this fun and interactive business game, you will learn:

- How to quickly raise your business income
- How business people can become rich and successful in a short space of time
- How to create a business that works without you

Isn't it time you had the edge over your competition?

Leverage has been played by all age groups from 12-85 and has been a huge learning experience for all. The most common comment we hear is: 'I thought I knew a lot, and just by playing a simple board game I have realized I have a long way to go. The knowledge I've gained from playing Leverage will make me thousands! Thanks for the lesson.'

Instant Success series.

INSTANT CASHFLOW
Turn every lead into a sale
(0-07-146659-2)

BILLIONAIRE IN TRAINING
Learn the wealth building secrets
of billionaires
(0-07-146661-4)

INSTANT PROFIT
Boost your bottom line with
a cash-building plan
(0-07-146668-1)

SUCCESSFUL FRANCHISING
Learn how to buy or sell a franchise
(0-07-146671-1)

INSTANT ADVERTISING
Create ads that stand out and sell
(0-07-146660-6)

INSTANT REFERRALS
Never cold call or chase after
customers again
(0-07-146667-3)

INSTANT LEADS
Generate a steady flow of leads
(0-07-146663-0)

INSTANT SYSTEMS
Stop running your business and start
growing it
(0-07-146670-3)

INSTANT TEAM BUILDING
Learn the six keys to a winning team
(0-07-146669-X)

*Your source for the strategies, skills,
and confidence every business owner
needs to succeed.*